FENG SHUI

 a beginner's guide

RICHARD CRAZE

Hodder & Stoughton

A MEMBER OF THE HODDER HEADLINE GROUP

Orders: please contact Bookpoint Ltd, 39 Milton Park, Abingdon, Oxon OX14 4TD.
Telephone: (44) 01235 400414, Fax: (44) 01235 400454. Lines are open from
9.00–6.00, Monday to Saturday, with a 24-hour message answering service.
Email address: orders@bookpoint.co.uk

British Library Cataloguing in Publication Data
A catalogue record for this title is available from The British Library

ISBN 0 340 73756 5

First published 1994
This edition published 1999
Impression number   10 9 8 7 6 5 4 3 2 1
Year   2004 2003 2002 2001 2000 1999

Typeset by Wearset, Boldon, Tyne and Wear
Printed in Great Britain for Hodder & Stoughton Educational, a division of Hodder
Headline Plc, 338 Euston Road, London NW1 3BH by Cox & Wyman Ltd, Reading,
Berkshire

CONTENTS

Chapter 7 Feng shui and the Inner
Good Fortune 88

Appendix 1
Feng shui and the I Ching 99

Appendix 2
Chart of directions and further
information 101

Appendix 3
The feng shui compass rings 102

Further reading 103

Glossary 104

The virtuous delight in mountains and hills;
the wise in rivers and lakes.

Chinese proverb

Have nothing in your houses that you do not know
to be useful, or believe to be beautiful.

William Morris

If you live in the Southern Hemisphere,
you will need to reverse all the compass directions given
in this book.

WHAT IS FENG SHUI?

*F*eng shui (pronounced *fung shoy*) is the Chinese system of arranging our environment so that we can live more in harmony with our surroundings. It means, literally, wind and water. It is an extremely ancient and well-developed system dating back at least 5,000 years and it has only been known about in the West for the last hundred. As more and more Western businesses find themselves trading with Chinese customers they are being persuaded to see the importance of feng shui: if your customers believe in it and you haven't incorporated its principles into your office premises then your Chinese customers simply will not do business with you.

AN INTRODUCTION TO FENG SHUI

Let's say you've decided to move house. You've been to all the estate agents in the area and collected several folders of property details. You've waded through them and drawn up a short-list of the ones you consider suitable. Then you've visited those houses and set your heart on one of them: the house of your dreams. It faces south, has a stream running across the bottom of the garden, has enough bedrooms and is quiet enough for the cats. All you have to do is make an offer, arrange a mortgage and move in. Oh, yes, you'd better get a survey done, right?

Well, if you lived in China . . . wrong. You wouldn't call in your surveyor but rather your feng shui consultant (*feng shui hsien-sheng*). They would come and see the house, take measurements

using a rather unusual feng shui compass called a *Lo-p'an*. Also they would need your birth date, place and time so they could draw up a detailed eight-point horoscope to see if you and your proposed dream house were compatible. And finally they would need a detailed report on all the previous occupants of the house, with a history of how their luck, wealth, health and happiness fared while they were living there.

When they had all the information necessary they would compile a report on the feng shui of your proposed purchase. This would include such details as:

- the *lung mei* (dragon's veins) of *ch'i* energy flowing in and around the building

- whether your family would prosper or decline there

- what changes you would need to make to increase your wealth there or to counteract any bad luck

- whether it was a *yin* or *yang* dwelling.

On the basis of their report, you would decide whether to buy the house or not. The Chinese consider it easier to put right construction faults than to buy a house that has a long-established bad feng shui because of its poor siting.

Even today Chinese people living in the West who want to buy property will baffle estate agents by asking more questions about who is living, and has lived, in the house for sale than they do about the actual house itself; after all they can see the building but they can't see the feng shui of the others who have lived there previously.

Simple remedies

So, what if the report is unfavourable? Well, don't worry too much. There are a lot of fairly simple remedies that you can carry out such as:

- hanging strategic mirrors to deflect *sha* (unhealthy energy)

- changing the layout of the garden

- adding or moving plants inside the house
- changing colour schemes
- using bamboo flutes, ribbons, statues and even electrical equipment to alter the flow of *ch'i*
- using wind chimes, flags and fountains to break up stagnant *ch'i*

So you can still buy your dream house, but you may have to do a little work before it has good feng shui.

What exactly is feng shui?

Well, it combines a unique blend of elements:

- magic
- divination
- interior design
- philosophy
- common sense.

It can be seen as an all-embracing view of the universe: heaven, the earth, people and energy, and it is used to predict and help change life situations such as your career, health, wealth, relationships and family life. For the Chinese it governs the location of their relatives' graves, where they live, the shape and ground plan of their houses, and decor. It can also be used to help determine lucky and unlucky days to begin a new building project, get married, arrange a funeral, start a new job or launch a business.

And the Chinese are very careful not to offend their neighbours' feng shui: they wouldn't add an extension, knock down a garden wall, alter a roof line or build a new house without first consulting everyone around the area. Roads and railway construction has often been delayed in the past in China because the proposed routes interfered with the feng shui of a neighbourhood. Even telegraph poles were objected to because of the way they disrupted the harmony of the landscape.

How can feng shui help us?

Whilst some parts of feng shui may seem irrelevant to us – siting of graves and layout of cities – there is much that has a sound practical application: office arrangements, interior design, furniture placements and garden layouts that could benefit us enormously. The Chinese have spent the last 5,000 years studying the psychology of human nature. Much of feng shui is using that study to help us to live more in harmony with our surroundings.

This book concentrates on the practical side of feng shui, with useful tips and advice on how to create healthy and harmonious living and working environments.

The history of feng shui

Feng shui has been around in China for at least as long as people have lived in houses. There are several very ancient books that outline its fundamental principles and explain its workings, ranging from the *Shih Ching* (Book of Songs) compiled between the ninth and fifth centuries BC to the *Li Chi* (Record of Rites) developed during the Han dynasty (206 BC – AD 220).

More modern works have included the *Ku Chin T'u Shu Chi Ch'eng* (Imperial Encyclopedia), a 1726 edition of which is in the British Museum, but the first reports of feng shui to arrive in the West were towards the end of the nineteenth century when missionaries first visited China on a regular basis. They were somewhat surprised to find that there was already an ancient and well-developed religion in place, *Taoism*, which was closely bound up with feng shui – and somewhat taken aback when they were not allowed to erect any Christian crosses. It was bad feng shui, they were told, to stab the land.

In mainland China, feng shui was practised extensively until Chairman Mao's Cultural Revolution which started in 1949 and lasted for nearly 20 years, during which all the old culture and ways were violently discouraged by the regime. Since the easing of government authority feng shui is making a rapid return.

Modern feng shui

In Hong Kong, Singapore, Taiwan, and other places without the oppression of the Cultural Revolution, feng shui has been practised continuously. Today it has a valid place in modern building design and feng shui principles have been included in the building of some important new sites including the Bank of China building in Hong Kong and the Hong Kong and Shanghai Bank.

The Hyatt Hotel in Singapore has reported a considerable upturn in business since it adapted its building to improve the feng shui.

Many businesses operating in both the East and West are seeing the value of its principles being incorporated into building design and decor. They include Citibank, Morgan Bank, Chase Manhattan and the Asian *Wall Street Journal* offices.

Who are the feng shui consultants?

In China they belong to several different types:

- Taoist priests who use feng shui in their religious practices

- geomantic divinators and fortunetellers who veer more towards the magical side

- true *feng shui hsien-sheng* who specialise in grave siting and complete house surveys.

In modern Hong Kong, and in the West, a feng shui consultant is likely to be part *hsien-sheng*, part interior designer and part esoteric practitioner. There is no formal training and the Lo-p'an compasses are hard to acquire in the West. A consultant may work on a very intuitive basis or take a lot of measurements and work out their report from them.

Selecting a consultant can only really be done by word of mouth: you can't tell how good or what sort they are from advertisements. However, there is nothing they can do that you can't learn to do for yourself once you have understood the basic principles and their practical applications. And it is about using your intuition – if you have ever felt uncomfortable sitting with your back to a door, or entered a strange house and felt instinctively that it was 'odd', then listen, as a feng shui consultant would, to your feelings.

pRACTICE

- What is an accurate translation of *feng shui* into English?

- Where would you go to find a consultant?

- How long has feng shui been known about in the West?

- If you used a surveyor in the West what would you use in China?

- Name two of the possible remedies against bad feng shui.

- What was the religion of China when the missionaries arrived?

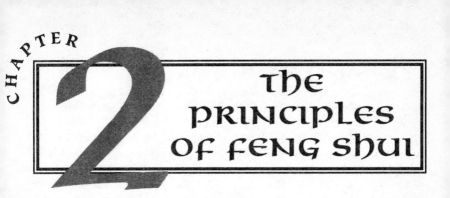

THE PRINCIPLES OF FENG SHUI

To understand the principles of feng shui we have to have an understanding of Taoism, the religion of China. Taoism comes from the Tao (pronounced: dow).

The Tao can be translated, and understood, as the Way. The Chinese say that everything is the Tao, everything is the Way. The Tao cannot really be likened to our Western concept of God, more to an idea of a fundamental inspiration from which everything in the universe flows.

From the Tao, the Way, comes everything we can know. That everything, according to the Taoists, can be divided into Heaven and Creation, or spirit and matter. They represented heaven as a circle, and creation, sitting in the middle of heaven, as a square, as in Figure 2.1.

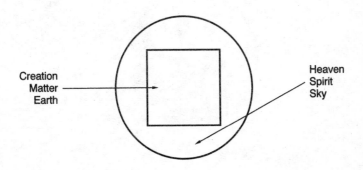

Creation
Matter
Earth

Heaven
Spirit
Sky

Fig. 2.1 *The square and circle. This shape is still used amongst the Chinese for lucky coins*

YIN AND YANG

From heaven, spirit, they reduced the circle to an unbroken line called *yang*, while creation, matter, became a broken line called *yin* (see Figure 2.2). The yin/yang symbolism was further developed into the most well-known of all Chinese symbols (see Figure 2.3). This is sometimes known as the *T'ai ch'i*, the Supreme Ultimate or the Great Art (not to be confused with Tai chi, the martial art/system of exercise which is more properly called *T'ai chi chu'an*, the great art of boxing).

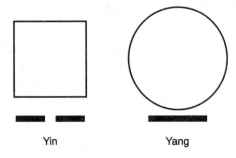

Yin   Yang

Fig. 2.2   *Yin broken line/yang solid line*

Fig. 2.3   *Yin/yang symbol*

From the Supreme Ultimate there comes the Tao, from the Tao comes yang and yin, and from those two opposites there is everything in balance. Although the yang and yin are opposites,

Yang	**Yin**
Sun	Shadow
Summer	Winter
Dry	Wet
Hard	Soft
Heat	Cold
Day	Night
Light	Dark
Creative	Receptive
Male	Female
Active	Passive
Positive	Negative
Sky	Earth
Heaven	Creation
Spirit	Matter
South	North
Up	Down
Outer	Inner

Fig. 2.4   *List of attributes of yin/yang*

within each there is always an element of the other. This is why there is always the tiny dot of white within the black yin, and the tiny dot of dark within the white of the yang. (See Figure 2.4.)

The yin/yang symbol should always be shown with the yin to the right as shown in Figure 2.3. This begins to give us compass directions. The light yang is at the top representing summer and the south while the dark yin is at the bottom representing winter and the north. All Chinese compasses are the opposite way round to those in the West: they have their south at the top where our north would be, and their west to the right and east to the left. (See Figure 2.5.)

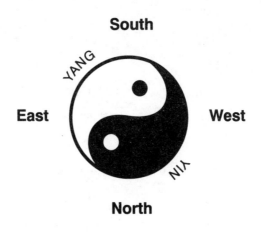

Fig. 2.5   *Yin/yang with compass directions*

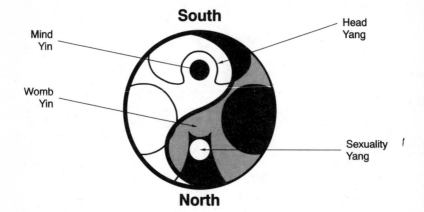

Fig. 2.6   *Yin/yang with human body*

The yin/yang symbol can also be used to represent the human body, with the head at the top representing spirit, yang, and the body below – matter, yin. Yang is the left-hand side of the body, while the right-hand side is female. (See Figure 2.6.) It is interesting that more and more research is being done in the West into the two brain halves: left brain controls the right side and would seem also to govern the more intuitive, artistic side of our nature and is known as the female brain, while the right brain controls the left side and governs our more mathematical thought processes, and is known as the male brain. Western science is just discovering this; it seems the Chinese knew it 5,000 years ago.

The four seasons

Using the yin, north, and yang, south we can combine these two symbols to create another two to represent east and west, spring and autumn, as in Figure 2.7.

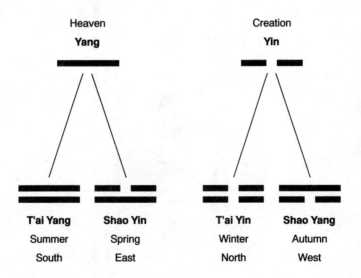

Fig. 2.7   *The two lines*

The Eight Trigrams

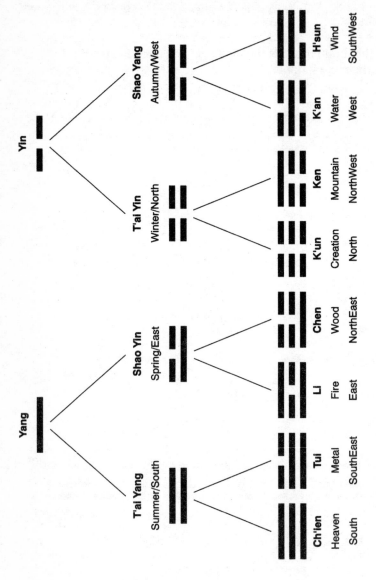

Fig. 2.8   *The Eight Trigrams*

From these four new symbols we can then produce another four to give us the rest of the compass and the mid-season points, as in Figure 2.8. These are known as the Eight Trigrams (a trigram is three parallel lines).

- The top lines represent the duality of heaven and creation – the yin/yang.

- The middle lines represent heaven and creation coming together to create the four seasons and the cardinal points of the compass.

- The bottom lines represent us, people.

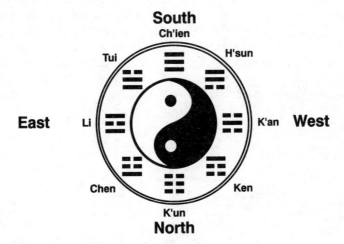

Fig. 2.9 *The Pah Kwa, the Great Symbol (Former Heaven Sequence)*

The eight trigrams are all named and have various significance and attributes. They are listed below, along with their Chinese name, its translation, their seasons, direction and main attributes.

- **Ch'ien** – *The Creative*, heaven, south, summer
- **Tui** – *The Lake*, metal, south-east, joy
- **Li** – *The Clinging*, fire, east, spring, the sun
- **Chen** – *The Arousing*, wood, north-east, thunder

- **K'un** – *The Receptive*, creation, north, winter
- **Ken** – *The Stillness*, mountain, north-west,
- **K'an** – *The Dangerous*, water, west, autumn, the moon
- **H'sun** – *The Wind*, gentle, south-west, wood

We can now form these trigrams into an octagon to give us the compass and the seasons. (See Figure 2.9.) This is known as the Pah Kwa, the Great Symbol, and is about as lucky a symbol as you can get for the Chinese. You will notice that south is at the top, as is correct for a Chinese compass, and north at the bottom.

The eight trigrams are thought to have been developed by Fu Hsi, a Chinese emperor, around 3,000 BC. It is said that he found them in the ornate markings on the shell of a tortoise which he studied on the banks of the Yellow River. The sequence in which he found them is known as the Former Heaven Sequence because around 1,000 BC they were rearranged into a different sequence called the Later Heaven Sequence (see Figure 2.10), by King Wen, a philosopher and founder of the Chou dynasty.

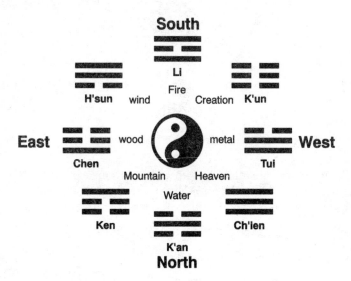

Fig. 2.10 *The Later Heaven Sequence*

feng shui and the I Ching

These eight trigrams can be paired into 64 new symbols (8 × 8) called hexagrams, which use six lines. These 64 hexagrams each have a meaning; Fu Hsi regarded them as an agricultural almanac which he called the *I Ching* (pronounced: *ee ching*), the Book of Changes. Bearing in mind that this was some 5,000 years ago, this is probably the oldest book in existence.

King Wen added to Fu Hsi's interpretations and turned it into the I Ching that we know today.

The I Ching and feng shui are closely related, as we shall see in later chapters.

The five elements

You will notice that the four cardinal points of the Later Heaven Sequence are also four elements (see Figure 2.11):

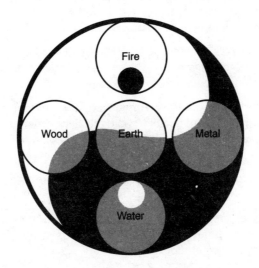

Fig. 2.11 *The five elements with earth in the centre*

- South/fire/*li*

- North/water/*k'an*

- East/wood/*chen*

- West/metal/*tui*

The fifth element occupies the centre and is earth.

Most oriental wisdom, medicine and philosophy is based on the Theory of the Five Aspects (*Wu Hsing*), which suggests that whilst we are a combination of all of the elements or aspects we do tend to display the characteristics of one more strongly than the others. These elements are not the elements of conventional Western astrology. It is better to regard them more as aspects of character.

Perhaps you would like to see which type you think you may be.

- **Earth** – *T'u* – The Diplomat – moderate, sense of loyalty, harmonious, likes to belong, pays attention to detail, likes company, needs to be needed, can be stubborn, should avoid damp.

- **Fire** – *Huo* – The Magician – compassionate, intuitive, communicative, likes pleasure, seeks excitement, likes to be in love, doesn't like to be bored, should avoid heat.

- **Water** – *Shui* – The Philosopher – imaginative, honest, clever, seeks knowledge, original, tough, independent, can be secretive, needs to be protected, should avoid cold.

- **Metal** – *Chin* – The Catalyst – organised, likes to control, precise, discriminating, needs to be right, likes order and cleanliness, appreciates quality, should avoid dryness.

- **Wood** – *Mu* – The Pioneer – expansive, purposeful, active, likes to be busy, can be domineering, needs to win, practical, should avoid wind.

Knowing which element you are – and if you've seen yourself in all of these above it probably means you're nicely balanced – will be helpful in your practice of feng shui.

For example a house that would suit a metal type would obviously be very different from one that would suit a wood type. It is also important to know which type your partner and/or children and anyone else you share your living space with is. It can help avoid a lot of conflict, and may well explain any difficulties, if you realise that each of the elements has contrasting responses to the others:

- **Earth:** helps metal, is helped by fire; hinders water, is hindered by wood.

- **Fire:** helps earth, is helped by wood; hinders metal, is hindered by water.

- **Water:** helps wood, is helped by metal; hinders fire, is hindered by earth.

- **Metal:** helps water, is helped by earth; hinders wood, is hindered by fire.

- **Wood:** helps fire, is helped by water; hinders earth, is hindered by metal.

You can see that two parents, one metal, one fire, living in a house with two children, one water, one wood, and an ageing earth relative will have to be incredibly accommodating if there is to be harmony.

Ch'i

We have looked at yin and yang, the seasons, the compass directions and the elements. There is one other component that we need to consider before we can move on to practical work, and that is the energy that binds them all together and flows within and around them. The Chinese call it ch'i (pronounced: *chee*) and regard it as the most important aspect of feng shui. When ch'i flows well there is good feng shui; when it stagnates it is bad feng shui. It can be seen as the underlying principle behind the Tao. Ch'i is the invisible force that animates everything, the life force. We cannot see, touch, taste, hear or feel ch'i, but we are aware of it by its effect. In acupuncture they say that there are four types of ch'i circulating in the body: Guarding, Internal Organ, Original and Protein. Creation is ch'i taking shape. When we die the living ch'i leaves our bodies. Is the departing ch'i the cause of death? Or does death force the ch'i out? Good question for the Taoists among us.

Feng shui can be seen as aligning our dwellings and ourselves to receive the maximum benefit of good ch'i. In Chapter 3 we'll see how it all works.

PRACTICE

- What is meant by yin and yang?
- What does the bottom line of a trigram represent?
- What is the luckiest symbol for the Chinese?
- What are the compass directions for the five elements?
- Which of the five elements is called the Philosopher?
- What is ch'i?

3 how feng shui works

*W*e've looked at the principles behind feng shui so now it's time to have a look at the actual mechanics: what you have to do to correct bad feng shui or improve good feng shui, and how you can determine what sort of feng shui you have in your office, house or garden.

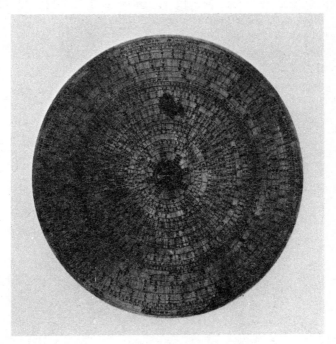

Fig. 3.1 *Feng shui compass. Reproduced by kind permission of the Whipple Museum of the History of Science, Cambridge.*

A Chinese feng shui consultant will use a feng shui compass (see Figure 3.1). This has a magnetic south/north needle at the centre with the emphasis on the south direction (a dot of paint, an arrow, a red line, etc.) whereas in the West it is the north direction that is given prominence. The south is always put at the top, which is the logical place really as it is also the yang direction which represents 'up' as well as 'heaven'.

Around the central compass is a series of rings (varying in number from 17 to as many as 36). Each of these rings contains information pertinent to the feng shui. The compass and rings are then set in a square base. The central rings are known as the Heaven Plate and the outer square is known as the Earth (or Creation) Plate. (See Appendix 3 for further details.)

The consultant will align the compass with the main direction the building (office, temple, grave, house, etc.) faces and read off the information that the Heaven Plate gives. They will then use a thin thread across the whole compass with a heavy weight that holds it in place to align the building with the horoscope of the person concerned. (See Figure 3.2.)

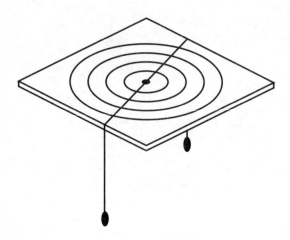

Fig. 3.2   *Compass in use*

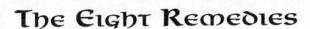

The Eight Remedies

Using both the compass and the thread will give two readings and, hopefully, they will be compatible. They rarely are, and so solutions have to be found to correct the feng shui. These solutions are known as the Eight Remedies and can be used in varying combinations depending on whether ch'i is to be stimulated, slowed down, encouraged or deflected.

- Light
- Sound
- Colour
- Life
- Movement
- Stillness
- Mechanical devices
- Straight lines.

Light

This includes lights, mirrors and reflective surfaces. Mirrors are probably the mostly widely known feng shui remedy. They can be used in most situations. They will reflect bad ch'i back out of a building, encourage good ch'i in by capturing a pleasant view from outside, lighten and enlarge small dark rooms, deflect ch'i around hidden corners, even alter and change the psychology of a room. Used in conjunction with lights they can transform a room completely. Lights should be as bright as possible without causing glare. The Chinese use a lot of lights outside of the house and in the garden to fill in missing or dead ch'i. This is not something we tend to make use of in the West but lights can enhance a dull garden, especially at night.

Sound

Most people would associate Chinese decor with wind chimes without realising that they are an important feng shui remedy. Anything that makes sound can also be used: bells, metal mobiles, bamboo tubes, etc. Melodic noises can help break up stagnant ch'i by causing swirls and eddies of sound in the air. Wind chimes also act as gentle alarms to tell us when someone has entered our house.

Pleasing and harmonious sounds are also good attractants of lucky ch'i: they are said to encourage wealth into buildings. The sound of water flowing is very beneficial. Fountains can be seen both as movement and sound.

Colour

The Chinese are great believers in using colour to stimulate the flow of ch'i, especially red and black. These are lucky colours associated with attracting wealth. In the West we usually prefer more subtle colour schemes but it is useful to remember that a sudden patch of strong, bright colour in a stagnating room can stimulate ch'i quite effectively.

Life

Plants are mainly used to fill in blank areas where there isn't any ch'i. They can be used to hide disruptive sharp corners that poke into rooms and stimulate ch'i in stagnant areas. Large plants can be used to slow ch'i down when it is being directed too quickly along straight lines. Fish in aquariums are also used for the same purpose. The Chinese word for 'fish' also means 'money', so they often use fish to represent wealth. That's why you will often see fish tanks next to the cash register in Chinese restaurants: it encourages you to spend freely.

Movement

Wherever ch'i needs to be stimulated or deflected use a moving object. The Chinese use flags, silk banners, ribbons, fountains, wind chimes, mobiles and weather vanes. Moving objects should use the natural power of the wind if possible and be made of natural materials.

The smoke from incense can be regarded as movement and be used beneficially, but obviously only in the short term. Flowing water brings ch'i to the building but it should move gently and gurgle rather than roar.

Stillness

Any large inanimate object such as a statue or large rock can bring a stillness to an area where ch'i is moving too fast. This is especially beneficial in gardens where the path to a front gate can cause the ch'i to leave too quickly. Any statues used should blend harmoniously into the landscape and have a particular relevance to the occupier. Statues of the Buddha work well for Buddhists, Pan for pagans and the Virgin Mary for Christians. The Taoists among us would probably benefit from a large natural stone object.

A small shrine, if you are so inclined, can generate stillness in a house and give a focal point to an area that needs lifting; it can also be a useful focus for our spiritual life which shouldn't be neglected.

Mechanical devices

In traditional feng shui this usually meant machinery but nowadays it can be extended to include any electrical equipment we need to use: televisions, stereos, electrical fans and, probably most important of all, computers. Electricity and ch'i need to be harmoniously regarded if they are not to clash: both need to be treated with respect. Electrical equipment can stimulate ch'i, but can sometimes overdo it, so keep it to a minimum. As we all live within a 'ring-main' we need to be aware of the effects electricity has on us and our homes. Keep it simple is probably the best advice for the practice of good feng shui.

Straight lines

The Chinese use flutes, swords, scrolls, bamboo tubes and fans to break up ch'i when it moves heavily or sluggishly, especially along beams and down long corridors. The straight lines are hung at an angle to create an octagonal shape (see 'Pah Kwa' later in this chapter) and that helps to direct the ch'i away from the beam or corridor and back into the rooms.

How and when you would use these eight remedies will be explained in later chapters.

The Four Animals of the Compass

The Chinese believe that buildings facing south have the best feng shui. They will always try to site their graves facing in that direction, so for the sake of simplicity we will assume for this chapter that you have a south-facing house. Don't worry if you don't; we will go into more detail about what to do in later chapters.

Each of the four cardinal compass points has been given an animal symbolism by the Chinese (see Figure 3.3):

- **South** – *Feng Huang* – the Red Phoenix
- **North** – *Yuan Wu* – the Black Tortoise
- **West** – *Wu* – the White Tiger
- **East** – *Wen* – the Green Dragon.

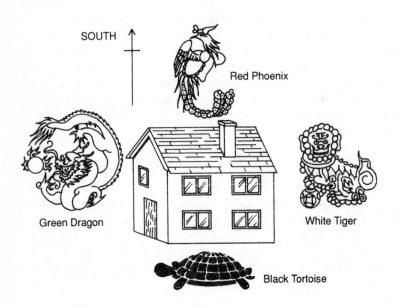

Fig. 3.3   *House surrounded by the Four Animal symbols*

The characters of the four Animals

Each of these animals has its own mythology and characteristics.

- **South** – the Red Phoenix (can also be pheasant, peacock, cockerel, crow, quail, or indeed any bird) – outward-going, lucky, summer, fame and fortune, happy, light, joyful, hopeful

- **North** – the Black Tortoise (can also be coiled snake, turtle, smoke) – sombre, hidden, mysterious, winter, sleepy, ritual, nurturing, caring

- **West** – the White Tiger – danger, unpredictability, suddenness, autumn, strength, anger, warfare, violence, might

- **East** – the Green Dragon – protective, good luck, kind, wise, spring, wisdom, cultured, good manners.

As you leave your front door (facing south) you will enter the realm of the Red Phoenix (yang). As you are out and about in the world this bird will bring you luck, wealth and fame. The Chinese always look for houses that have front doors that open to the south-east to let in both the luck and wealth of the Phoenix and the wisdom and protection of the Dragon. The land in front of your house should fall away gently, not too steeply or the Red Phoenix will fall off, and not too flat or your worldly success will stagnate.

To the back of your house is the Tortoise area of mystery and nurturing (yin). This is where you would look for aspects of your marriage, children and close family. There should be hills behind you to help keep secret and loved all that is precious to you.

To the west of your house should be the flat, low area of the White Tiger (big yin/little yang). If you have hills or even, heaven forbid, mountains to the west, the White Tiger will prove to be too strong, and unforeseen calamities will befall you. If the land falls away too steeply the Tiger will be small and your life will be boring and predictable.

To the east, where the sun rises, should be the green hills of the Dragon (big yang/little yin), a place of rejuvenation and hope. This is where you would look for your experience, wisdom and learning. The Green Dragon protects scholars, writers and artists.

This, then, is the ultimate house. Ideally there should be a stream coming from the north-west – blocking the unpredictable ch'i of the Tiger – and flowing down across the front of the house – bringing life to the Red Phoenix – and disappearing off to the south-east. The stream should meander and there should be waterfalls (small ones). Figure 3.4 illustrates this perfect location.

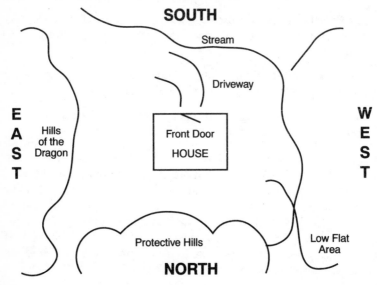

Fig. 3.4 *The perfect location*

Pah Kwa, the Great Octagon, and the Eight Enrichments

If your house doesn't face south, rest assured. Each direction enriches the household in a different way:

- South – *Wang Ts'ai* – prosperity and fame
- South-east – *Huan Lo* – wealth and money
- East – *Fa Chan* – wisdom and experience
- North-east – *T'ien Ch'ai* – children and family
- North – *Chin Yin* – successful relationships
- North-west – *Chin Ts'ai* – new beginnings, improvements
- West – *Chang Yin* – pleasure and indulgence
- South-west – *An Lu* – peace and happiness

These eight directions and enrichments can be added to the Pah Kwa octagon (see Figure 3.5), which can then be overlaid onto any house plan. A feng shui consultant would know these eight directions off by heart and could come into your house and suggest improvements just by seeing what you had in each area.

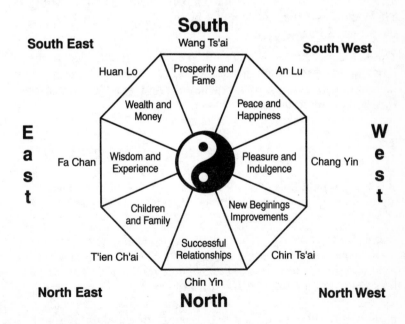

Fig. 3.5 *Pah Kwa with the Eight Enrichments*

They might look and see that your desk, computer and textbooks were all in the Chang Yin area. How could you ever expect to get any work done if whenever you sat down to study or write you were in the 'pleasure and indulgence' area of your house – probably a better place to have your kitchen.

When you overlay the Pah Kwa onto your house plan it should always be facing south even if your front door does not. Note that your house faces whichever way the most important (probably largest) door is facing. Even if you always use a back door, or come in and out through the garage, your house faces in the direction of your front door. If you choose not to use it and use another door instead then there may well be a feng shui reason for this.
Maybe your front door opens in the T'ien Ch'ai, the area of children, and as a single person you find that confronting, so you choose to use your side door, which is in the Chang Yin area of pleasure and indulgence. If you're single, there's no problem. However, if you're part of a loving couple desperate for children and living in a similar location, and you notice you have a partner who uses the Ch'ang Yin side door all the time, could it be that one of you isn't as desperate as they make out?

This is the mechanics of feng shui. We will do the practical in the next few chapters. In the meantime you can draw up a ground plan of your house, office, garden or whatever and then we can overlay the Pah Kwa onto it.

Lo Shu, the magic square

If you extend the Pah Kwa out into a square you will be able to divide it up into nine equal sections. This is the beginnings of the Lo Shu, the magic square (see Figure 3.6).

In each of the nine squares you can enter one of the enrichments with the centre left blank (see Figure 3.7). Each of these squares has a number from 1 to 9. If you add up three numbers in any straight line, up or down or diagonally, you will arrive at 15 – a magic square indeed. The Lo Shu is a very ancient Chinese charm and many buildings in China (and the city of Beijing) are build according to its principles.

South
Wang
Ts'ai
Huan
Lo
An Lu
Fa Chan
Chang Yin
T'ien
Ch'ai
Chin
Ts'ai
Chin Yin

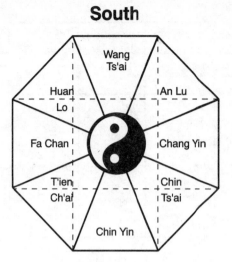

Fig. 3.6 *Lo Shu: the magic square*

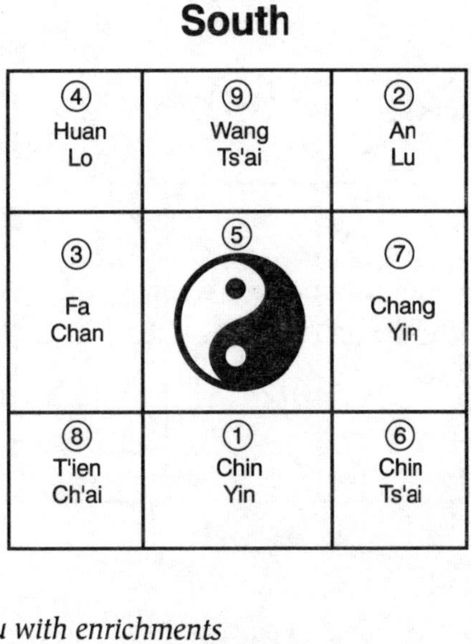

South
4
Huan
Lo
9
Wang
Ts'ai
2
An
Lu
3
Fa
Chan
5
7
Chang
Yin
8
T'ien
Ch'ai
1
Chin
Yin
6
Chin
Ts'ai

Fig. 3.7 *Lo Shu with enrichments*

South

9 - 11am May **Snake**	11am - 1pm June **Horse**	1 - 3pm July **Sheep**
7 - 9am April **Dragon**		3 - 5pm August **Monkey**
5 - 7am March **Rabbit**	☯	5pm - 7pm September **Chicken**
3 - 5am February **Tiger**	11pm - 1am December **Rat**	7 - 9pm October **Dog**
1 - 3am January **Ox**		9 - 11pm November **Pig**

East ... **West**

North

Fig. 3.8   *Lo Shu with times and animals*

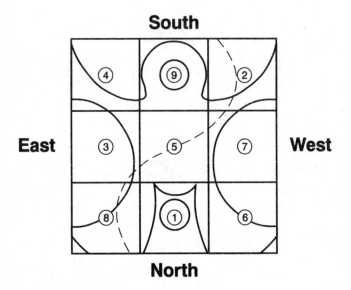

South

East ... **West**

4   9   2
3   5   7
8   1   6

North

Fig. 3.9   *Lo Shu with human body outlined*

The Lo Shu will also give you times of the day, seasons, and even the Chinese astrological animals (see Figure 3.8). If you want to take it even further you can add parts of the body (see Figure 3.9).

The real use of the Lo Shu, however, is a very important part of feng shui called 'Walking the Nine Palaces'. This is a ritualistic way of checking the feng shui of your office, house or garden. You should always begin at 1, the front of your building, and follow the walk in the sequence outlined below of 1 to 9, ending up at 9, the back.

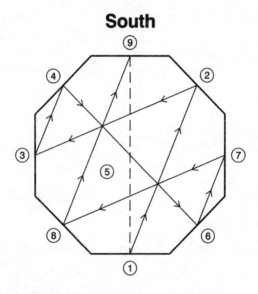

Fig. 3.10   *Lo Shu with Pah Kwa*

The Nine Questions

As you walk into each enrichment area check the Nine Questions:

- How does it look?
- How does it feel?
- What furniture is there?

- What is its decor like?

- What do you use the area for?

- What could you change?

- What could you improve?

- What do you like?

- What displeases you?

We will deal with the practical side of Walking the Nine Palaces in later chapters when we look at individual locations in more detail.

When you finish the walk, crossing back from 9 to 1, ideally you would now be facing the south looking out of your front door or front gate. If you find you are looking in another direction don't panic. It can depend a lot on which of the five aspects or elements you feel you are.

- *Facing south* – ideal for water, not bad for wood, ambivalent for metal and uneasy for fire.

- *Facing north* – ideal for fire, not bad for metal, ambivalent for wood and uneasy for water.

- *Facing east* – ideal for wood, not bad for fire, ambivalent for water and uneasy for metal.

- *Facing west* – ideal for metal, not bad for water, ambivalent for fire and uneasy for wood.

The other directions will be a mixture of the cardinal points. A house facing south-west could suit both water and metal and be uneasy for fire and wood, while a house facing north-east would be helpful for fire and wood types and uneasy for water and metal.

And what about you earth types? You've hardly had a mention. Well, that's because you're so well balanced you barely need feng shui (although your house may well do). You can live almost anywhere. It doesn't matter what direction you face – you are the centre, the heart of any home. You should avoid high-rise blocks, however. Earth types do well in basements. In fact they are the only type that do. Earth types should avoid extremes, maintain balance and enjoy harmony in everything.

Matching homes and aspects

Sometimes a feng shui consultant can be called in and – without even getting their compass out or taking any measurements or even thinking about Walking the Nine Palaces – will pronounce a judgement about the feng shui of the house. That is because sometimes a house will be so glaringly at odds with its owner that it can be immediately diagnosed as being unsuitable. Each aspect or elemental type has a correspondingly suitable house type:

- Fire – comfortable, intimate
- Wood – practical, unusual
- Earth – harmonious, family
- Metal – modern, ordered
- Water – period, conservative.

That about covers the mechanics of feng shui. The next chapters will look at how we put it all together into a practical package.

PRACTICE

- What are the Four Animals?
- Which compass directions do they govern?
- Make a ground plan of your office, house or garden.
- Check the compass direction of your house to see which way it faces.
- Name two of the Eight Remedies.
- What direction do the Chinese think of as most favourable?

4 FENG SHUI IN BUSINESS

Who hasn't dreamed of opening and running their own business? We know we need cash flows, budget forecasts and business plans for the bank manager, but in China a prospective entrepreneur may also be asked for the feng shui of their proposed new business. Is the site auspicious? Is the feng shui good? What of the history of the past occupants? Were they lucky and healthy there?

The Chinese and superstitions

The Chinese are a very superstitious race and a lot of their beliefs may seem confusing to us. For example they won't use the number 4 for a shop if they can avoid it, because it sounds too much like their word for 'death', and the number 2 sounds like 'and again' – so *424 the High Street* would be a most unlucky address for them. It sounds too much like 'death and death again'. We may think this an irrelevant superstition but if we went to China and opened a business at that address we would quickly go bankrupt. Why? Not because 424 holds any magical power, but because our potential customers would not come in because *they* think the number is unlucky.

However, if you opened the same business in the West, and at the same address, your customers would not know of 424's unpleasant connotations (unless they were Chinese of course) and would flock in (you hope), making you very rich. Thus, many of the Chinese interpretations and translations of feng shui make little sense to

Westerners. In this book I have tried to include only the practical side, the parts that will make sense because they are based on some sound psychological reason or genuine common sense. It wouldn't mean a lot to us to be met with the Chinese greeting of 'may your wallet always be full of fish!' unless we knew Chinese. Fish, as you may remember, is slang for cash.

SITING YOUR BUSINESS

The Chinese attach far greater importance to ancestor worship than we do. They are far more concerned about the trappings and rituals of death than us. They would never consider for a moment that a business could flourish in the same street as an undertaker's while we would probably not even notice. They would consider it a very bad omen if a hearse stopped outside your business for a moment on its way to the cemetery. And as for opening a business overlooking a graveyard – forget it! So I will deal with good and bad sites only on their logical merits.

LOOKING FOR PREMISES

When you have decided what type of business you are going to run you begin to look for premises. Your Chinese feng shui consultant would come with you to check the neighbourhood. You can simply do this for yourself. Supposing you wanted to take over an existing shop. We may consider it unnecessary to find out about the previous occupants: but if you think about it, it is actually a very logical thing to do. It makes sense to enquire. For instance if the previous owners had run the business for 30 years and were retiring to their country cottage after a successful and rewarding career it is auspicious for you. However, if the last three owners had all gone bankrupt, you might be well advised to look elsewhere.

It is also logical to look at the shops or businesses that will be your neighbours. Are they clean and busy? Do they look successful and thriving? Are the shop fronts inviting or dirty and dingy? Try to look at the shop-front as a customer – would you want to go in?

If you are going to rent a suite of offices where clients will visit you it is important to look at the entrance. Is it welcoming? Could it be improved? How would you brighten it up? Could you make it more agreeable?

This may not sound like feng shui to you but I can assure you it is all part of it. It is an important area, and one that many people overlook when opening a new business. Maybe feng shui could be summed up by saying it is a ritualistic way of making you stop and think about what you are doing rather than rushing in, as many of us do, in the first heady excitement of buying a new business.

We also need to look at the location with regard to its road access. Chinese believe that ch'i follows roads, and indeed follows anything that runs in channels or lines – which is why engineers had so much trouble when they first tried to put up telegraph wires in China because of the way it affected everybody's ch'i (and the poles stabbed the land, which wasn't a good thing either).

Roads and ch'i

If roads channel ch'i it makes sense to use this knowledge to our advantage. Roads aimed directly at our business will channel the ch'i too quickly (see Figure 4.1). The Chinese call it *killing ch'i* because it directs too much ch'i at us, too quickly.

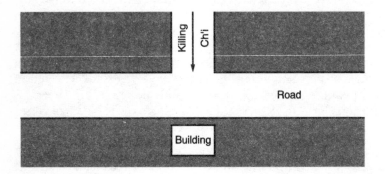

Fig. 4.1   *Killing ch'i road*

What is even worse than killing ch'i is *arrowed killing ch'i*, where two or more roads form a point or arrowhead aimed at our business (see Figure 4.2).

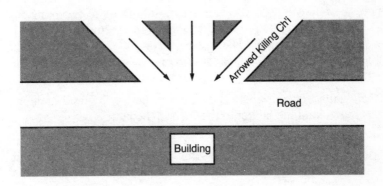

Fig. 4.2   *Arrowed killing ch'i*

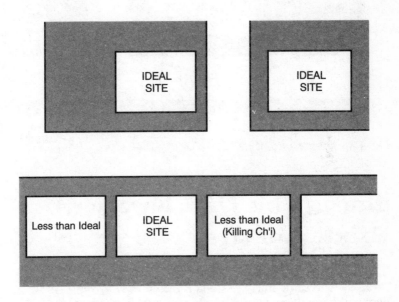

Fig. 4.3   *Ideal site*

If your business is faced with an arrowed killing ch'i it can make you defensive, even paranoid. You need to hang a mirror facing outwards to deflect the ch'i. The best type of mirrors are octagonal ones that reflect the shape of the Pah Kwa. These can be hard to get hold of in the West, so you can use ordinary square or oblong ones. These are fine for the purposes of deflecting ch'i, but even better would be a round one. Make sure it is completely flat as concave and convex mirrors are used for other purposes. More about that later.

The ideal site is one where the road runs across the front of your business – and the nearer to the corner, the better (see Figure 4.3).

If you have managed to acquire the corner site you have to pay some attention to your main entrance. Which side would you put it? Ideally it should cut across the corner, as in Figure 4.4.

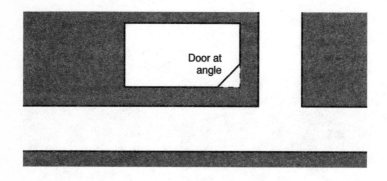

Door at angle

Fig. 4.4   *Corner entrance*

Using the Pah Kwa with Enrichments

Now is the time to have your ground plan ready. Overlay on it the Pah Kwa with Enrichments – don't forget to have *Wang Ts'ai* (Prosperity and Fame) to the south – and you should now be able to see where to put the cash register – *Huan Lo* (Wealth and Money) of

course. You may well be better off putting the staff restroom in *An Lu* (Peace and Happiness) rather than *Chang Yin* (Pleasure and Indulgence) otherwise you'll never get them out and back to work!

Always remember that ch'i likes to flow in gracious curves and feels unhappiest flowing in straight lines – it makes it hurry – so plan your entrance and/or reception area bearing that in mind. Does the entrance open into the reception in an inviting way, or is it a harsh, sudden transition? If it does seem harsh, use wind chimes to break up the eyeline and create a softer approach.

Using your discretion

If you're worried about what the customers will think of your experiments in feng shui, then find less confronting alternatives. Octagonal mirrors may need a word of explanation but an ordinary one wouldn't. Wind chimes may appear oriental but a hanging banner proudly carrying your company logo could be an asset. If you want to be a secret feng shui practitioner – and some do – then you have to put in a bit more thought and work. Fish tanks are very oriental, especially near the cash register, but an ornamental fountain will seem much more Western. I had to work with a business in Bristol where some of the clientele were Chinese but th majority were not. The business needed a remedy in its *Fa Chan* area (Wisdom and Experience) which coincided with the reception. It was a new business and ch'i was stagnating there. I knew they would react if I suggested anything too oriental so I compromised and recommended a small fountain set in a pool containing some conventional goldfish with a few ferns and rocks. It was duly installed and the Chinese were impressed that the management had considered them important enough to improve the feng shui, while the Western clients were fascinated by such an unusual decor addition. Business improved. I also managed to get some ceiling fans installed – I told the management it would help circulate the heat – but it was actually to stop ch'i collecting and stagnating in an otherwise too high ceiling. So you can practise feng shui and still be discreet. On the other hand it does provide a good conversation piece for your customers, and maybe makes them feel a little bit special that you've taken some effort over them.

OFFICE LAYOUTS

One of the most important accessories to any office worker or manager is the humble desk. We spend a lot of time behind them and yet probably give little thought to their position. Desk siting is a very crucial aspect of good feng shui in the office. Ideally the desk should face the door, as in Figure 4.5, not force us to sit facing away from the door as in Figure 4.6. We all know the feeling of someone coming up behind us and making us jump, so it is best if we can see their approach. The Chinese talk about adopting 'a superior attitude' which gives them an advantage in business negotiations. Seeing someone approach gives them time to adopt the superior attitude but it may be simpler than that – just good psychology: to be able to see the room laid out in front of us allows us to feel in control. As a door opens we need to be aware of what is going on around us. Despite our 'civilised' evolution we still have our 'flight or fight' responses.

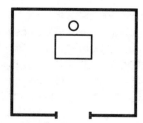

Fig. 4.5   *Well-positioned desk*

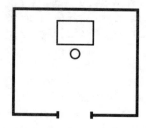

Fig. 4.6   *Badly positioned desk*

If you try to remember the Pah Kwa as much as possible it makes siting of desks or any other furniture that much easier. Ideally a desk should be placed diagonally across the corner of the room facing the door, as in Figure 4.7. Arranging furniture diagonally across corners is probably something quite alien to Westerners – we do like to put things against walls – but once you have tried it, and lived with it for a short while, it begins to feel very odd putting everything back in a straight line.

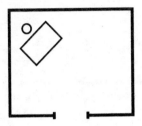

Fig. 4.7   *Desk in Pah Kwa*

If two people have to share an office they can both face the door and still create a pleasing Pah Kwa shape by utilising the opposite corners, as in Figure 4.8.

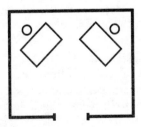

Fig. 4.8   *Two desks in office*

If you have a lot of desks to take care of, say in a typing pool, try to break up the straight lines as much as possible. Remember ch'i likes to move around things, not flow too quickly along channels. (See Figures 4.9 and 4.10).

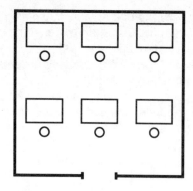

Fig. 4.9   *Badly positioned typing pool*

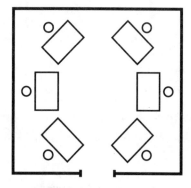

Fig. 4.10   *Well-positioned typing pool*

If you have a worker who likes to leave early or makes excuses and is absent a lot, look at the siting of their desk. You may well find that it will be near to a door (probably the one that takes them home). Resite their desk away from the door and, to break the habit they may have acquired of thinking about leaving all the time, try to site it out of sight of the door.

If you cannot position your desk facing the door but are obliged for whatever reason to have it facing a wall then you should make use of the mirror remedy. Position a mirror so that you can see the door, as in Figure 4.11. This also helps give the office a more spacious feel and amplifies light.

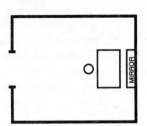

Fig. 4.11   *Desk facing a wall*

You can also use mirrors to reflect a pleasant view into the office.
The Chinese will always try to reflect water into the office to
encourage ch'i to flow. Water is also calming and inspiring. You
have to spend a lot of time in an office, so it makes sense to make it
as harmonious as possible.

CORRIDORS, WALLS AND DOORS

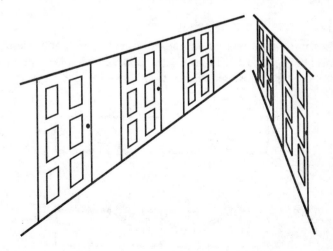

Fig. 4.12   *Long corridor*

The long, bleak corridors that seem to be a design fault of so many Western office buildings (see Figure 4.12) unhelpfully encourage ch'i to move too quickly. This is why a lot of offices seem to cause a feeling of lethargy in those who work in them: the ch'i is always rushing away. To slow it down it is necessary to break it up by using wind chimes, banners or straight lines across it, as in Figure 4.13.

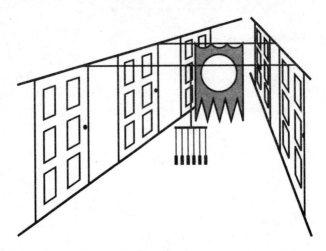

Fig. 4.13   *Long corridor with remedies*

Doors should face each other and not be just out of alignment, as they are in Figure 4.14. To rectify the offset doors, place small mirrors on the opposite walls, as in Figure 4.15.

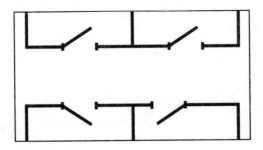

Fig. 4.14   *Doors opposite and doors offset*

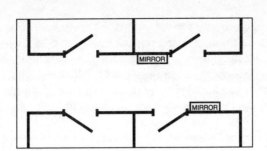

Fig. 4.15 *Offset doors with remedy*

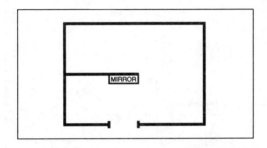

Fig. 4.16 *Doors opening onto walls, with remedy*

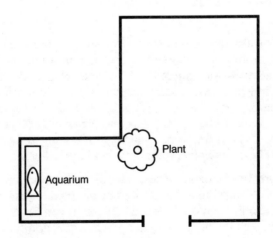

Fig. 4.17 *Corner with plant*

Doors should open into the room and not onto walls. If they do you will need to use the mirror remedy, as in Figure 4.16. Walls that jut into offices will need to be softened with plants. Tall plants will help break up the sharp ch'i, as in Figure 4.17. Alcoves and corners can be lifted with lights and plants to discourage the ch'i from stagnating and get it moving back into the room, as in Figure 4.18.

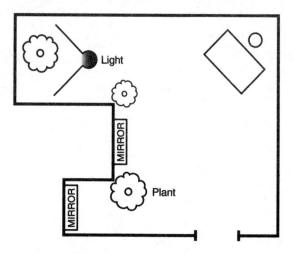

Fig. 4.18   *Corner and alcove, with remedy*

Large blank walls can be uninspiring for office workers to have to look at all day long, so break them up with a mirror or use, as the Chinese do, scrolls with calligraphy. You may wish to be discreet about this, in which case display tasteful water-colour prints instead. Bear in mind that we have to spend a lot of time in our work-place. It has to be harmonious and pleasant or ch'i cannot thrive. Lack of ch'i is the same as lack of life – your workers will not give of their best if they feel unhappy – and nor will you.

This is a fairly brief look at offices. A lot of the information in the next chapter, 'Feng shui at home', can be adapted for use in the office. But before we go on, let's see how much you have remembered – all the answers to the practice questions are in this chapter, somewhere.

PRACTICE

- What is 'killing ch'i'?

- Draw up a Pah Kwa with Enrichments for your office.

- Where does the area of Huan Lo fall? What have you got there?

- Walk the Nine Palaces of your office.

- Where is the ideal site for your desk? Move your desk to different positions in your office and spend some time just sitting there seeing how you feel. Check against the Pah Kwa to see in which area of enrichment you've got your desk. Could you improve on the position, perhaps by moving it from T'ien Ch'ai to Wang Ts'ai?

5 feng shui at home

*A*s we spend most of our time at home it makes sense to ensure that it is as pleasant and harmonious as possible. In the West we use decor and interior design to help us to do that, while in China they use feng shui as well. They are as concerned as we are to ensure that the visual impression is pleasing but they also like to make sure that the energy flow in and around the home is as beneficial as possible.

Key areas to check

There are a few key areas that need checking when we apply feng shui to our homes. If we work through them in order it will make it easier for you to remember when you come to apply the principles to your own home.

- Mountains – *shan*
- Surroundings – *hsueh*
- Water – *shui*
- Wind – *feng*
- Trees – *liu*
- Dwelling – *chai*
- Inside – *fang*
- Ourselves – *hsin*

Mountains and surroundings

Even if we do not live near a mountain range the principles of *hsueh* can still apply, especially if we consider any tall buildings near us as 'mountains'. Their towering presence can overpower our ch'i. Concave and convex mirrors can turn their image upside down, which will negate the effect of their powerful ch'i. Similarly the reflection from a bowl of water will have the effect of flattening their image.

Any tall buildings should ideally be in the Tortoise and Dragon areas, to the north and east. If they are not, you will have to use mirrors to make flat areas in your Phoenix and Tiger areas, south and west. Place small mirrors in the window facing outwards.

Hsueh, surroundings, means checking the immediate neighbourhood for good or bad feng shui. What are the neighbours like? Are there ugly buildings quite close to you? You need to look out from the four cardinal points of your home to see what is there.

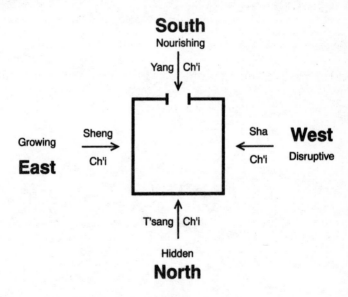

Fig. 5.1 *House, checking the directions for ch'i*

You also need to check the four types of ch'i that may be directed at your home. They are:

- **Sheng ch'i** – growing ch'i from the east

- **Yang ch'i** – nourishing ch'i from the south
- **T'sang ch'i** – hidden ch'i from the north
- **Sha ch'i** – disruptive ch'i from the west.

You need to stand outside your home in each of the four cardinal compass points and look to see what is there (see Figure 5.1).

South

For example you may stand with your back to the side of the house that faces south and find yourself looking at a particularly unpleasant factory. Is this really where you want your nourishing *yang ch'i* to be coming from? And the side of the house facing it? Is it your main entrance or a blank wall? If it is blank then the factory ch'i will not do too much damage.

East

Stand and look east from where the *sheng ch'i* is coming. This ch'i stimulates you, gives you your creative energy. So what's there? Another factory? A splendid view of rolling hills? Which would you prefer?

North

And to the north? The *t'sang ch'i*, hidden ch'i? This is the sleepy stuff that you can roll up in and hibernate. Ideally it should undulate down from the tortoise hills in a gentle embracing way. What have you got there?

West

And west? This is the *sha ch'i* that we've mentioned before. It is disruptive and unpredictable. The Chinese sometimes even go so far as to say that it is dangerous and destructive. Where's your *sha ch'i* coming from? And how's it getting into the house? The main entrance or a back door that you hardly ever use? If it's the main entrance, you need to deflect it fairly firmly. Use the largest mirror you can on the inside wall immediately opposite the door so that the *sha* is deflected straight back out again. If it's a back door you can use a smaller mirror or wind chimes to break up the *sha* as it enters. If you don't use the door too much then there is less need to deflect the *sha*. And what windows open onto the west? Have a look and decide how much *sha* can get in through them. You can deflect it by hanging those small balls of glass in the window. I'm sure you know the ones I mean, those that spin round on thread and give off prisms of colour as they catch the light. The Chinese traditionally used to black out any west-facing windows.

Terraces

Obviously if you live in a semi-detached or terraced house you can't do this test on all walls. If you live in a terrace then the ch'i coming from your neighbours is important. You can also go to each end of the terrace and see what is coming towards the whole line of houses.

Tower blocks

If you live in a block of flats or high rise building you have the added complication of what is coming up. Maybe you live above a shop. What sort of shop? What sort of ch'i is filtering up through your floors? The Chinese would never live above a funeral director's but they might be very happy to live above a bank.

Basements

Living in a basement, a very yin place, needs consideration as to what is above you. Again it may be shops, other flats, even a police station. The Chinese feel that any place that may have been subject to emotional distress, like a police station, a prison, army barracks or hospital, gives off a particular type of ch'i called *fan ch'i*, translated as offensive ch'i, and that it can be quite harmful, causing you to feel the same emotional distress as was originally generated.

Earth types often do well in basements.

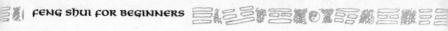

feng shui and harmony

A lot of feng shui is intuitive work. I can't give examples of every
type of house and the direction it could face. You have to look
yourself and feel whether the energy is right. A lot of feng shui is
also common sense. If every time you open your front door you are
confronted with a dreadful view you are bound to feel worse than if
you look out on a wonderful vista of countryside, streams and
beautiful hills. Your quality of life improves with the quality of your
horizons. 'But we can't all look out on such a splendid view,' I hear
you say. 'I look out onto a prison and a railway station, I can't help
that!' Well, you can actually. Feng shui is also about taking
responsibility. We all choose where we live. Feng shui is partly
about waking up to that choice. We can improve it but ultimately
you may have to move if you come to realise that where and how
you live is adversely affecting your emotional and spiritual horizons.

Some people, however, can resist negative forces better than others.
You're perfectly entitled to live opposite a factory if you choose –
just be aware that you're making that choice.

We need to look for harmony in our lives, to seek out the natural
and the nurturing. If we choose to live in an inner city surrounded
by derelict buildings, busy polluted roads and millions of other
people, then we are going to feel the effects that all that negative ch'i
generates. If we choose to live in the countryside in quiet, tranquil
surroundings with beautiful views, then we will benefit. Obviously
there has to be, as in all things, a question of balance. There will
always be a time in our lives when we need the excitement and
stimulation a city offers and a time when we need to get away from
it all. Judging when those times are is up to you. Only you can tell
when you have had enough and need to recharge. A lot of people
don't even think about the alternatives. Feng shui is about seeking
that balance, that harmony.

Water and wind

We need water around us. If we are not lucky enough to live near
rivers and streams then we have to add the water ourselves. That's

why aquariums are so important to the Chinese (as well as the fish – money pun).

Water carries ch'i as well as being a soothing element of our environment. If there are rivers and streams near us we need to look at the way they bring ch'i to us. Using the principles that we have already learnt we can work out which are good and bad. Ch'i, which is beneficial, likes to meander; *sha*, which is disruptive, likes to travel in straight lines. So, does the river head straight for your home or wander happily around it? Is it a gently babbling brook or a concrete banked canal? Guess which carries ch'i and which carries *sha*. It's time for you to do some work now.

Do you look out over a lake? Large bodies of water such as lakes, reservoirs, even large ponds, accumulate ch'i. Is it overwhelming? Even worse, is it in the west? A lake here would store *sha* in large quantities and would almost certainly be an extraordinarily powerful force that would erupt unpredictably. Is the lake in the north? This could make you very sleepy indeed.

We need water in the home and if we can use mirrors to reflect watery views inside, so much the better. The sight and sound of water moving naturally can be most beneficial and soothing.

Trees

The Chinese term here is *liu*, a direct translation of which would actually be 'willow'. This is the tree most often represented in traditional Chinese landscape paintings (which are called *shan-shui* incidentally). If we see buildings as the yang element of the landscape then trees are the yin: and we need both for our spirit to be nurtured. The shan-shui painters work on a ratio of 3:2: three yang elements to two yin. They also see, as do feng shui practitioners, hills as yang and hollows as yin. If you take a panorama, three-fifths should be yang, the sky, and two-fifths yin, the landscape. We can use yin trees to balance an excess of yang buildings or yang hills. In the West this ratio is known as the 'golden section', and it is as important in Western art as it is in Eastern.

Liu, trees, can also be understood as 'garden'. The garden is quite a large subject on its own so it gets its own chapter, the next one, 'Feng shui in the garden'.

Dwelling

This is the feng shui of the actual building itself: the walls, the windows, the doors, the rooms and the decor. We can look at this in greater detail shortly.

Ourselves

There is little point in getting the feng shui right if the heart of the home also needs work doing on it. We can see ourselves as the heart. We need to be as in balance as our home. Getting the feng shui right can make quite a difference but we also need to sort out our own personal feng shui. We are the recipients of all that good ch'i. Do we make good use of it? Are we following the Tao or swimming upstream? Are we a help or a hindrance? Part of the solution or part of the problem? Only you can answer these questions – it's not a test.

Room by room feng shui

Assuming you have your own home and are not looking to move at the moment then we need to work through the feng shui of your home in an ordered fashion. Here is a checklist to remind you:

- The Four Directions
- The Five Elements
- The Eight Enrichments
- The Nine Palaces
- The Nine Questions
- Rooms
- Decor
- Furniture

We will take it step by step.

front door

Let's start at the very beginning. What sort of front door have you got? Is it in proportion or too large, allowing too much ch'i to escape? If the latter, the remedy is to hang a wind chime to divert the ch'i back in. If it is too small, than hang mirrors either side to give the illusion of it being bigger.

What direction does it face? What sort of ch'i is it letting in? There are eight remedies and you can use any combination of them to improve the feng shui. Remember also that you can do no harm; you can only improve the feng shui, because you are using natural cures. The worst you can do is keep things as they are.

Entrance hall

If you have an entrance hall, see it as a pause before you enter or leave the home proper: a moment to reflect. How you spend your moment depends on the nature of your hall. What's there?

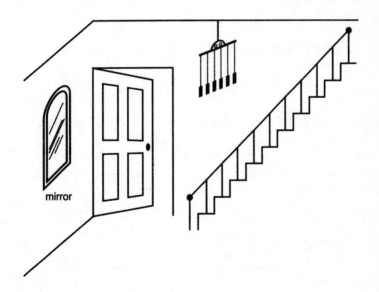

Fig. 5.2 *Stairway into hall, with remedies*

If you have a staircase does it directly face the front door? That will allow the ch'i to rush straight down and out.

Remedy: wind chime hanging above the bottom step will slow the ch'i or a mirror strategically placed to divert the ch'i (see Figure 5.2). Does the hall have windows? Windows allow ch'i to circulate: without them it can stagnate.

Remedy: use mirrors to reflect a window view into the hall from an adjacent room and leave the door open to allow the ch'i to flow. By now you should be able to identify the problem areas and intuit the remedy required.

SITTING ROOM

Apart from the bedroom this is probably where you spend most of the time in the home. You need to check which of the Eight Enrichments your sitting room falls into. Hopefully it will be the An Lu, peace and happiness – although of course you will also need to know which element you are for this to be true; fire types could well prefer it to be in Chang Yin.

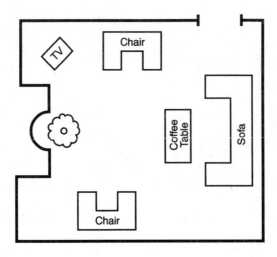

Fig. 5.3   *Sitting room before rearrangement*

Furniture should be arranged so that the 'honoured guest' position faces the door. The honoured guest position is the best one – the most comfortable chair, the one nearest the fire. Honoured guest position is usually the one we have ourselves, the one we least like to give up when friends call round. Make sure it faces the door in the same way you would with your desk in an office. The rest of the furniture can feel most comfortable when it follows the Pah Kwa shape of the octagon. (See Figures 5.3 and 5.4.)

Watch out for corners jutting into sitting rooms as well as dead corners and alcoves.

Remedy: use plants to allow the ch'i to flow around corners harmoniously and not too straight. Alcoves can be enriched with lights, plants or aquariums. (See Figure 5.5 overleaf.)

Some sitting rooms have the dining area, or indeed the kitchen, adjoining them. It is best if these are not seen first when the door to the sitting room is opened. If they are, they should be screened with a plant-covered trellis of some sort.

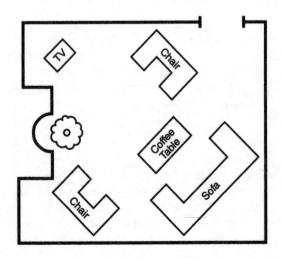

Fig. 5.4 *Sitting room with Pah Kwa furniture arrangement*

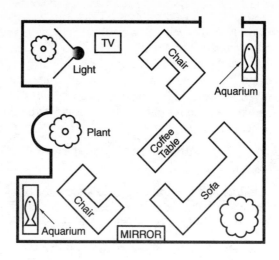

Fig. 5.5   *Sitting room corners remedied*

Sitting rooms should be comfortable but not too crowded: you need to allow the ch'i to flow or you can feel lethargic if the room is too full of furniture, ornaments and clutter.

Heating is important to us in the West, where we suffer extremes of weather, and the focal point of any Western sitting room was always the fireplace until the television invasion. If you regard a fire as a movement remedy and a television as a mechanical remedy you can see that perhaps we have unbalanced our sitting rooms. Maybe we need to restore that balance. We don't give our other electrical appliances such prominence: we merely use them as and when we need to and then put them away.

Perhaps our televisions (this goes for stereos as well) would be better housed in cupboards and watched when needed. Then when they were not needed they could be discreetly hidden away. Then the fireplace could take up its proper focal position once again. In some Mediterranean countries the fireplace is positioned in the corner of the room, as in Figure 5.6. This is sound feng shui as it curves the corner, allowing ch'i to circulate, and also adheres to the octagon.

Fig. 5.6   *Corner fireplace*

Kitchen

If the sitting room is the heart of the home then the kitchen is the lungs: this is where the breath and inspiration of a home should come from. This is the room that can benefit most from good feng shui. As you have to work at counters, sinks and cookers, it is invariable that carrying out some tasks will cause you to have your back to people coming into the kitchen. You need to be aware of this and incorporate as many mirrors as is necessary to overcome it. You will find that mirrors, as well as correcting the feng shui, will also give the illusion of greater space and increase the light available.

Some people don't like mirrors in their kitchen, especially if they live in a period house, because of the modern look they can create. You can always do what a friend of mine does, and that is to use lots of reflective surfaces instead – line up your stainless steel toaster, your shiny expresso machine and your kettle to act as mirrors – it works just as well. This is good kitchen design as well as good feng shui. (See Figures 5.7 – 5.10.)

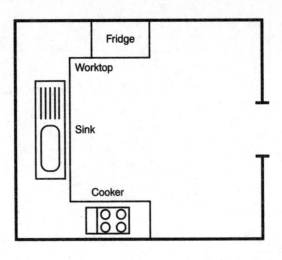

Fig. 5.7   *Kitchen before re-designing*

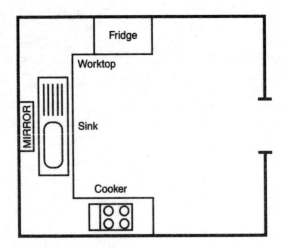

Fig. 5.8   *Kitchen after re-designing*

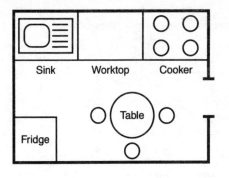

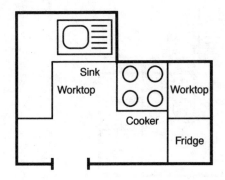

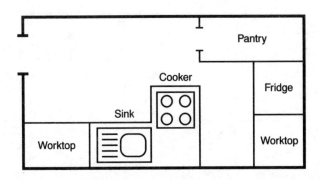

Fig. 5.9   *Three kitchen plans*

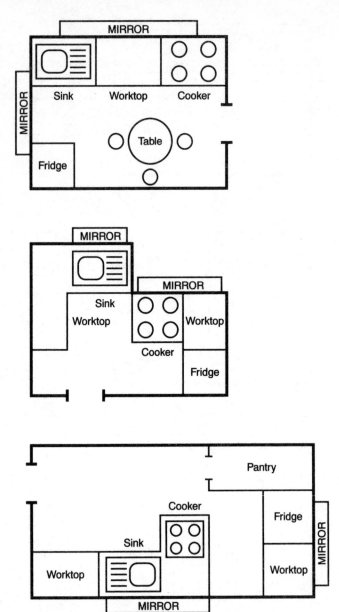

Fig. 5.10   *Three kitchens after re-design*

Dining rooms

The same rules apply to dining rooms as to sitting rooms. Make sure the furniture allows the ch'i to flow easily and harmoniously around the room. Honoured guest position should face the door. Try not to have the door opening too close to any chairs. Ideally the table should incorporate the Pah Kwa shape but as we cannot all have octagonal tables you will have to try to incorporate the shape into the place settings or the chair arrangements or even an octagonal flower bowl or vase. (See Figures 5.11 and 5.12.)

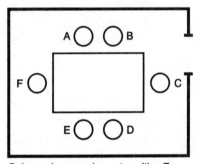

Only one honoured guest position F
Door too close to C

Fig. 5.11   *Dining room before rearrangement*

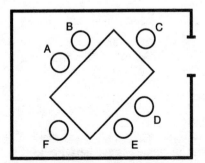

Now two honoured guests A and B
Door equidistant from C and D

Fig. 5.12   *Dining room after rearrangement*

STAIRS

Staircases allow the ch'i to flow up to the upper floors but also down from them. If the stairs are too close to the front door then the ch'i will flow down and straight out. The upstairs rooms will feel drained and empty if this is the case. Breaking up the flow of ch'i with a wind chime or even a well-placed plant could be beneficial here.

Stairs with bends in them can help the ch'i to flow well as it likes to curve and meander. However, if the bend is too sharp or severe then the ch'i will not be able to turn properly.

Remedy: a small mirror strategically placed.

Spiral staircases present special problems. If they have open treads then the ch'i will fall straight through, like water down a drain.

Remedy: fill in the treads if you can; failing that, try placing a small mirror face-up underneath the stairs to reflect some of the ch'i back upstairs.

Spiral staircases are a problem even if they don't have open treads as they are so nice and curvy that the ch'i disappears too quickly down them.

Remedy: try growing a vine up the main central support. If that is impractical paint the stairwell pale green. Failing that, place a small mirror underneath them, or try a hanging remedy such as a wind chime half-way down.

The clue with stairs is to stand at the top and then at the bottom and imagine yourself to be the ch'i. Ask yourself where you would flow, how quickly, what you would encounter and what would help you.

BATHROOMS

The Chinese believe that a toilet with its seat-lid left up will allow ch'i to vanish down the waste pipe. Keep the lid down. Make sure the bathroom is not in your Wang Ts'ai area, prosperity and wealth. If it is, it is even more important to heed the warning about leaving the seat-lid up. Keep the bathroom door closed as much as possible and hang a mirror on it facing outwards.

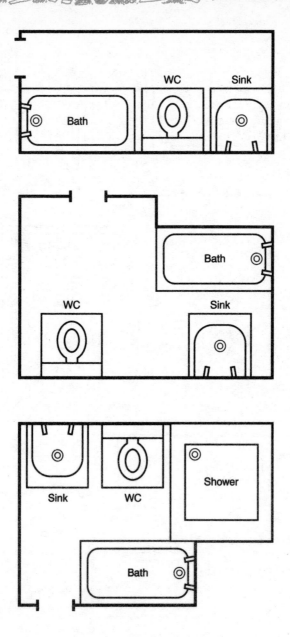

Fig. 5.13 *Bathrooms before rearrangement*

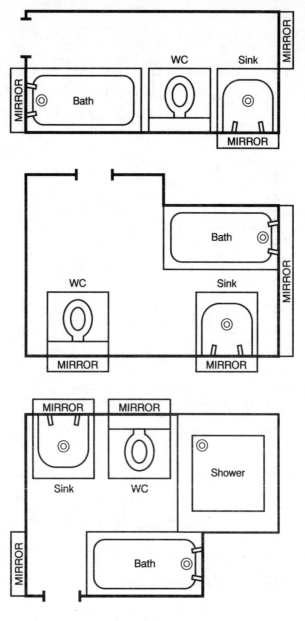

Fig. 5.14   *Bathrooms after rearrangement*

A friend in the music business, Tim Freke, who had struggled for years to get a recording contract, was issued with one the day after he carried out these remedies to his own bathroom. Coincidence? Another friend had a troublesome teenager. Her downstairs cloakroom is in the T'ien Ch'ai. She keeps the toilet lid down and installed a mirror – no more problems with her son.

Make sure that the same rules apply in the bathroom as in the office: make sure that whatever you are doing you can see anyone coming in; if you are in the bath even with the door locked you should be able to adopt 'superior attitude' if disturbed. The same goes for sitting on the loo! The toilet shouldn't be the first thing you see when you open the door: very bad feng shui. If it is you can hang a mirror behind it or a hanging remedy such as a wind chime in the door entrance to distract the person as they enter. (See Figures 5.13 and 5.14.)

Corridors and Landings

Long corridors can funnel ch'i too quickly.

Remedy: break them up by hanging something across them: banners, wind chimes, etc.

Small, fore-shortened corridors can be expanded with a mirror on the end wall or either of the side walls or even ceiling.

Landings should ideally be light and airy. If not, try leaving a suitable landing door open and reflecting a pleasant light view with the strategically placed mirror.

Bedrooms

Bedrooms probably deserve a feng shui book all to themselves. As we spend maybe a third of our lives in this one room it is obviously important to get it right.

Check in which area of the Pah Kwa with Enrichments your bedroom falls. If it's not right, can you move it or change over with another bedroom? Failing that, you can use the Pah Kwa on just the bedroom and make sure your bed is placed in a more auspicious position.

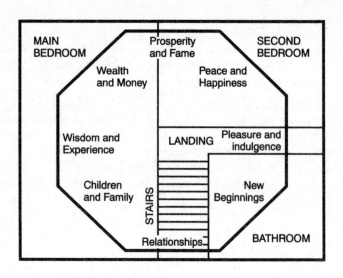

Fig. 5.15   *Upstairs plan with Pah Kwa*

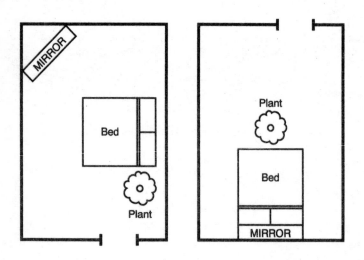

Fig. 5.16   *Bedroom furniture placement, with remedies*

Can you see from the example given in Figure 5.15 how overlaying the Pah Kwa on an upstairs floor plan can highlight potential problem areas? What would you anticipate might be the effects brought about by having Chin Ts'ai, new beginnings, in the bathroom? What would you do about it?

Check the view from the bedroom window and use strategic mirror placements if possible to reflect water or trees into the room (see Figure 5.16).

Try not to position the bed with the foot facing the door if you can: the Chinese say that this is the way dead people are laid out prior to being removed from the house – they are always carried out 'feet first'. However, you do want to be able to see who is coming in, so use the octagonal shape again wherever possible (see Figure 5.17).

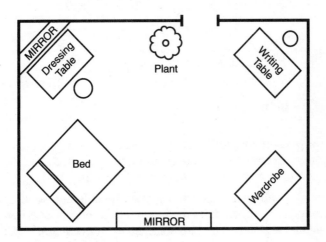

Fig. 5.17   *Bedroom furniture with Pah Kwa*

WINDOWS

Ideally windows should open outwards. Arched or octagonal windows are good feng shui. Windows with sashes that slide up and down are not particularly helpful as they can never be opened entirely. Unless you change them (and if you live in a Georgian

Fig. 5.18   *Sash window, with remedy*

house that may not be feasible) you need to encourage the ch'i to enter and leave smoothly; open the top half and place plant arrangements in the bottom half, as in Figure 5.18.

If windows open inwards, check which of the different ch'i they are letting in. Opening inwards to the west could prove inauspicious so take remedial action by blocking excess *sha* ch'i with a mirror, a plant on the window sill, or a hanging wind chime. You might even have to put up a blind and keep it permanently pulled down.

Doors

Doors (see Figures 5.19 and 5.20) should open opposite each other and not be offset. If they are, use a mirror remedy as in office feng shui.

Try not to position furniture too close to inward-opening doors.

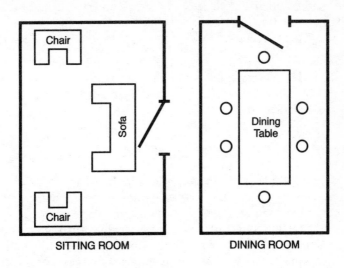

Fig. 5.19 *Furniture and doors before rearrangement*

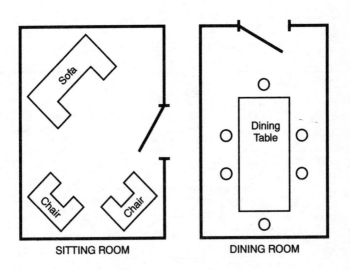

Fig. 5.20 *Furniture and doors after rearrangement*

Doors should open and close easily. If you have to push or pull hard to close a door, think what the ch'i has to do. Oil the hinges and allow easy access. Squeaky doors should be treated the same.

Doors should be in proportion to the room size. Too large and they allow the ch'i to escape; too small and they restrict the ch'i entering. You need to slow down or encourage the ch'i respectively. Use suitable remedies.

Roofs

We have a great love of exposed beams in the West – something the Chinese are not so familiar or so comfortable with. They believe that ch'i can travel too quickly along beams. Suitable remedies are anything that slows the ch'i down. You may like to adopt their cure, which is to tie red ribbons onto the beams or use the 'straight line at an angle' approach. This involves using two bamboo tubes or flutes placed across the beam at an angle of 45 degrees to create the Pah Kwa shape. (See Figure 5.21.)

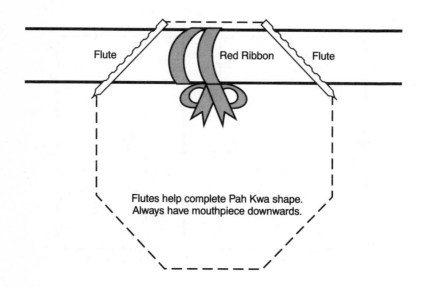

Fig. 5.21   *The beam remedied*

The Chinese also feel that beams can cause an oppressive weight above us if they are exposed. If they are above our heads when we are sleeping or sitting down then they may cause headaches; over our stomachs and they cause digestive problems.

Large beams over windows in the form of lintels can block the ch'i. You need to remedy their effect with red ribbons, hanging lamps or wind chimes, even trailing vines along them – anything to break up their hard, sharp lines.

I think we have gone through the house in a fairly comprehensive way. Obviously I cannot give examples of every type of room or furniture. Good feng shui practice is as much about using your intuition as it is about following a ritual. Once you have learnt the basic principles you can implement them if you are prepared to be mentally flexible and take your time to consider the problem from more than one angle.

- Avoid straight lines.

- Encourage gentle curves.

- Look to see where the ch'i is coming from.

- Imagine you are the ch'i.

- Keep everything as natural as possible.

- When in doubt use the Pah Kwa.

PRACTICE

- In order, check: Mountains (*shan*), Surroundings (*hsueh*), Water (*shui*), Wind (*feng*), Trees (*liu*), Dwelling (*chai*), Inside (*fang*), Ourselves (*hsin*).

- Draw up a ground plan of your home. Overlay the Pah Kwa on to it. See where the Eight Enrichments are. Walk the Nine Palaces and check the feng shui of each one. Check the four cardinal points for the type of ch'i.

6

fENG shuI IN The GARDEN

*O*ur garden is like our aura: it can tell our visitors a lot about us before they've even met us. What sort of impression do we want to give? What sort of ch'i comes in? How harmonious is our garden?

DRIVEWAYS AND ENTRANCES

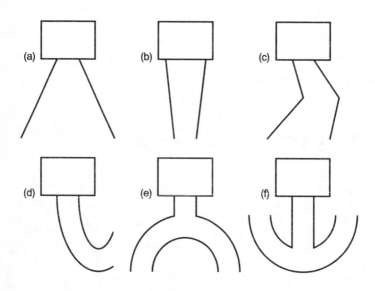

Fig. 6.1   *Different types of drives: a, b and c are difficult feng shui while d, e and f are beneficial*

The driveway (see Figure 6.1) can be seen as a ch'i funnel. Too straight and it will encourage *sha*. If it narrows as it gets nearer to the house it can concentrate ch'i too intently. If it widens towards the house it can weaken ch'i.

Again you need to see from which direction the ch'i comes: which type; *sheng, yang, t'sang* or *sha*.

Imagine you are the ch'i: what effect will you have?

Ideally you should be looking for a wide, curving drive that swings around towards the house from the south-east. The driveway, ideally, should slope away gently. If it is too steep, luck and money, it is said, will roll away. You can always install posts or pillars just before the drive drops away too steeply and this will remedy it. A light here will also help.

Horseshoe-shaped drives are very good, allowing the ch'i to arrive and depart harmoniously.

When you make out your ground plan, remember to include the garage. Some people drive straight into their garage and then enter the house by a side door instead of using their main entrance. This can affect the ch'i balance of the whole house by causing the occupant to adopt a smaller attitude to their outside affairs. A light installed between the garage and the house, pointing upwards towards the roof of the house, will help alleviate this imbalance.

If you park in the road and have a garden path then the same rules apply for them as do for drives. Check the funnelling effect of the ch'i.

If the path is very narrow and straight it can restrict the flow of ch'i, making you feel subdued before you even enter the house. The width of the path should be in proportion to the width of the main entrance; not too wide, nor too narrow. It should curve gently towards the main entrance. Paths that run along the side of the house can unbalance the ch'i, almost confusing it so that instead of entering the dwelling it will carry on past, leaving the house feeling deadened and cold. Again, imagine you are the ch'i – does the house invite you in or would you want to go straight past? Do you feel able to flow harmoniously or are there too many right angles and straight lines?

Paths in the back garden

Again you need to check the direction the ch'i is coming from. Paths from the west should undulate as much as possible to minimise the effects of the *sha*. Paths from the south can run straighter and truer as you may well wish to encourage the yang ch'i, nourishing ch'i from the south. A back garden path leading from the south usually means a north-facing house, which can feel sleepy. You need to encourage all the invigorating ch'i possible.

The garden

Try to see the garden (see Figures 6.2 and 6.3) as the yin element of your dwelling and the house as the yang. You then have two opposite aspects, the female and the male. Houses tend to have hard, sharp lines and your garden can have as many soft, rounded curves as you like.

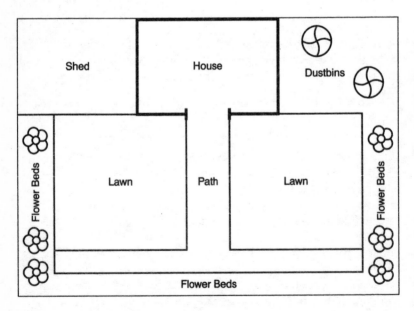

Fig. 6.2 *Garden before re-design*

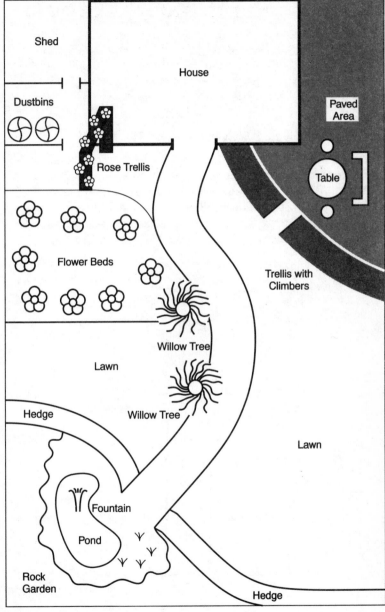

Fig. 6.3 *Garden after re-design*

In the West we do tend to go in for oblongs of lawn with straight paths forming the edges, straight flower beds and a very open outlook. The Chinese tend to go more for rounded paths, curved flower beds, and lots of secret hidden bits so that as you follow a path you can turn a corner and find a scene or a view that you hadn't expected. Like the yin element it is more secretive and hidden, alluring and beguiling.

The courtyard garden

Even with small courtyard gardens we can do a lot to encourage ch'i to wander and meander peacefully. Again we need to imagine we are the ch'i. What will encourage us to stay? How do we feel happiest? By being the ch'i we will get an excellent idea of what is wanted. And as humans are living manifestations of ch'i, what is good for the ch'i is also good for us. (See Figures 6.4 and 6.5.)

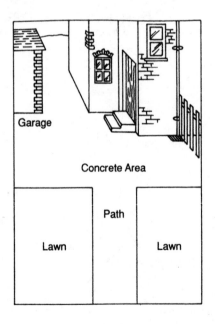

Fig. 6.4   *Courtyard before re-design*

Climbers

Gravel

Weeping Tree

Flower Beds

Brick Patio

Lawn

Fig. 6.5   *Courtyard after re-design*

FOUNTAINS AND PONDS

The Chinese consider a garden without water to be a garden without life-blood. Water encourages ch'i to circulate and remain. Only in the grandest of Western houses do we tend to see an abundance of fountains, and yet even the smallest and most humble dwelling could benefit from the judicial placing of a small pond complete with working fountain. Electric pumps that circulate the water are now so cheap to buy from garden centres and household stores that it seems a meanness not to give ourselves the pleasure that such a small investment could provide. Moving water enriches our lives in much greater quantities than the cost of installation. It seems such a small investment that one wonders what else one could spend one's money on that would yield such a vast return of happiness. Moving water encourages wildlife, restores our equilibrium, soothes our spirit and constantly recharges the ch'i. Who could ask for more? (See Figures 6.6 and 6.7.)

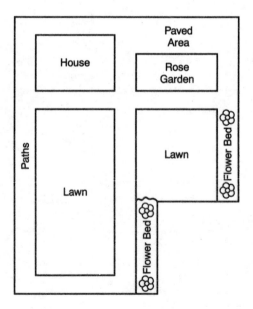

Fig. 6.6   *Garden without water*

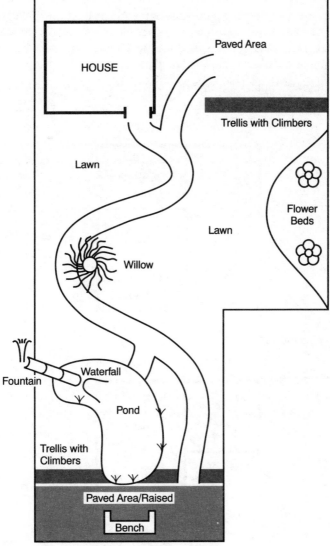

Fig. 6.7 *Garden with water*

Tbe OuteR Good foRTUNe

If you have drawn up your ground plan (see Figure 6.8), you will, hopefully, have included the garden. If not then you had better do it now. Once you have, then it's time for the *'Outer Good Fortune'*. This is just a fancy translation of how to feng shui your garden.

From your ground plan join up any diagonal lines that cross over outside the house (see Figure 6.9).

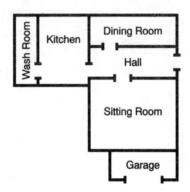

Fig. 6.8   *Ground plan*

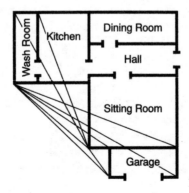

Fig. 6.9   *Ground plan with diagonal lines*

These lines crossing indicate areas that need to be looked at. These are the areas where you can use fountains, statues or large stones, or even plant a tree (see Figure 6.10). This will encourage your good fortune. (We will look at the Inner Good Fortune in the next chapter.)

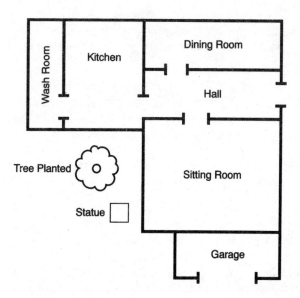

Fig. 6.10   *Outer Good Fortune completed*

If you look at any houses painted in the Chinese landscape style, or even at photographs of Chinese architecture, you may well notice that the roofs curve upwards at the corners. This is to soften the hard edges and allow the ch'i to flow more smoothly. The Chinese hang wind chimes from these upward curves to encourage the ch'i. If you implement the upward curve in your garden design you won't go far wrong. Allow everything to flow gently, without hard edges.

Try to avoid any hollows if you can. The Chinese believe that the *ts'ang-feng*, a cold hidden wind, blows from them and can cause ill health.

Trees

Trees should be soft and allow your eye to be led harmoniously through the garden. Some trees have a harsh outline and should be avoided: conifers, firs, cypress; while others are naturally more gracious and yin: willows, maples, tulip trees, magnolias, weeping purple beech.

The tall, angular types like conifers should be avoided unless you happen to live in a high mountainous region. Go for the softer ones if you can.

Beware of cutting down any mature trees. They have been there longer than you and have developed their own relationship with ch'i: it has grown used to flowing around them in a particular way and will not like being disturbed. The more ancient and gnarled a tree is the more you should be wary of removing it. If it has become an eyesore or is an unproductive fruit tree you can liven it up by allowing a suitable climber to cover it.

Rock gardens

If you remember the four cardinal directions and the four symbolic animals that accompany them you will find it easy to work out where the raised areas in your garden should be. The Chinese use rock gardens to build up any flat areas that could benefit from a more yang approach. I'm not going to tell you where or how, because by now you should have absorbed the basic practices and principles.

Climbers

Climbers like wisteria, clematis and Virginia creeper can be used to break up the hard edges of the house to allow the ch'i to flow more harmoniously, as well as providing colour and interest. You can use Russian Vine if you want to cover walls quickly, but keep it away from your roof.

Fig. 6.11   *House without climbers*

Fig. 6.12   *House with climbers*

Paved areas

We need paved areas to sit out in the garden to enjoy the sunshine, relax, eat with friends or just dream away an hour or two. Obviously these areas should be fairly close to the house so we don't have to carry the tea tray too far and yet we don't want to be too close to the telephone and other distractions. As with all things a balance has to be found. The paved area can be screened from the house to give it a secret feel, making it a private place where we can relax and be ourselves without visitors intruding on us and taking us unawares.

The paving itself can be arranged in whatever pattern we want but try to avoid the overly straight lines that *sha* likes so much. Bricks laid in a herringbone pattern create a delightfully colourful area. Or paving slabs laid out in the Pah Kwa shape can be just as restful.

Large areas of paving can look bleak unless they are mellowed with small plants and they help break up any *sha*. Use thymes, thrift, saxifrages, dianthus. The thymes don't mind being walked on.

It is best to break up very large areas of paving with shrubs and small trees planted in an irregular pattern.

The Chinese also regard smell as very important: that's why they usually go for the more fragrant blossoms such as wisteria, buddleia, lilac, jasmine and honeysuckle. Ch'i will flow with pleasant smells, *sha* will flow with unpleasant ones. Good ch'i flowers are: lilies, lotus, lavender, sweetpeas, pinks and any of the yellow roses.

Hedges and screens

Hedges can create delightful secret areas. Avoid the too neatly pruned ones as they only encourage *sha*. It is better to go for a more natural look, with beech and other wide-leaved plants. Let hedges wander in curves, if you can – straight lines look too artificial.

Screens can be created using bean poles and then training fruit trees or climbers up them. The Chinese are very fond of the ubiquitous bamboo, which will grow in the West just as easily and can provide a haven for wildlife as well as acting as an efficient windbreak.

Arbours can be created with a simple framework and a suitable climbing plant. A garden bench set in an arbour makes a tranquil place to relax and enjoy the sunshine.

As this is a book for beginners, and garden feng shui could occupy a whole book all on its own, I will trust that I have given you enough basic information to be able to work out the feng shui of your own garden and how to improve it. You have to do some of the work, you know!

PRACTICE

- Draw up a garden plan. Where does your garden ch'i come from? Where do your paths face?

- Draw up the Good Fortune guide. Do you need to correct any feng shui? How will you do it?

- Why do the Chinese value water in the garden?

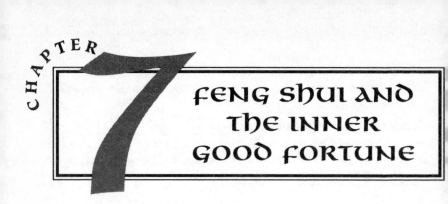

7 FENG SHUI AND THE INNER GOOD FORTUNE

The lessons we are going to learn in this, the last chapter, are about the Inner Good Fortune which can be applied to any dwelling, although it best helps correct the feng shui of odd-shaped rooms and ground plans. We will also work through two case studies to see how we put it all into practice.

CASE STUDY 1

This is a converted chapel set in rural surroundings. Most Chinese would not choose to live in a chapel as they tend to think of them in the same way as churches, which they avoid because of the graveyards. However, this one is all right because it has never been used for burial services. It has no graveyard. It is on a split level with steps from the entrance hall and kitchen up to the living room. It has the bedroom and bathroom above the entrance hall. There is a small back garden but no front garden – just a car parking space. It was built around 1760 and was converted into a house about ten years ago. The ground plan is shown in Figure 7.1.

As you can see it is a very irregular shape which causes all sorts of feng shui problems. We will work through it logically.

- Draw up the ground plan.

- Ascertain the compass direction of the house from the entrance.

- Overlay the Pah Kwa shape on the ground plan.

- Join the Eight Enrichments to the centre of the Pah Kwa.

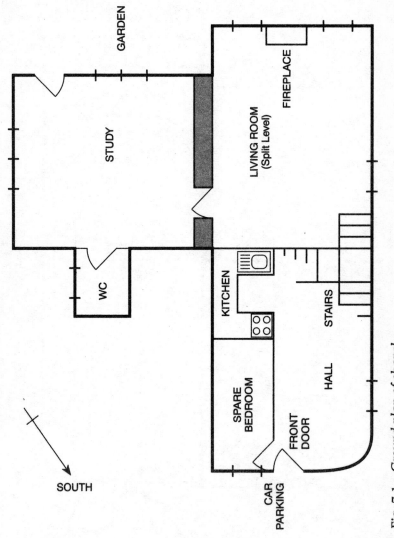

Fig. 7.1 *Ground plan of chapel*

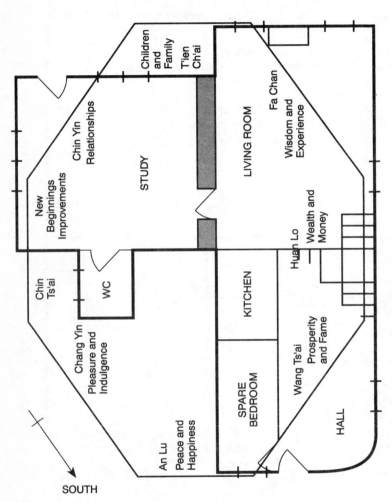

Fig. 7.2 Chapel ground plan with Pah Kwa

- Mark with a cross any disturbance in what should be eight perfect triangles.

- Use mirrors on any cross on an outside wall.

- Use plant or other remedy on any inner crosses.

Ground plan and compass direction

You should by now have had some practice in drawing up a ground plan. Figure 7.2 shows the plan for the chapel. It faces south-west. We can find this out by taking a compass direction from the front door.

Overlaying the Pah Kwa shape on the ground plan

Remember that the Pah Kwa always has its south in the correct position – facing south. If you have an odd-shaped building like this one then you have to extend the whole ground plan mentally into a larger shape so you can see where the Pah Kwa fits. It should occupy a central space and take in at least two of the furthermost apart outside walls that are opposite each other. You will notice that the ground plan of our chapel (Figure 7.2) has some missing areas and some extra areas.

Missing areas

If you look at the diagram you will see that the outside walls cut into the Chang Yin, pleasure and indulgence, and the An Lu, peace and happiness. The first could be seen as a good thing but it may make for a somewhat serious person; the latter could make for someone striving continually for career and advancement. There is also a piece missing out of Chin Ts'ai, new beginnings and improvements. This could lead someone to overlook opportunities and find making changes difficult.

There are also gaps in the children and relationship areas. In both

 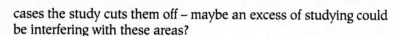
cases the study cuts them off – maybe an excess of studying could be interfering with these areas?

Extra areas

There is quite a large extra piece tacked on to Wang Ts'ai, prosperity and wealth, and also on Fa Chan, wisdom and experience.

Is any of this telling you what sort of person lives here? Or what sort of person would be ideally suited to live here? Actually it's quite a good match. The chapel is owned by a single professional writer in her early thirties. She works extremely hard and is very successful, both financially and in status. While not yet ready to settle into marriage and have children, she is looking to do that in a few years. If that happens then the chapel may have outlived its usefulness and she may find it beneficial to move to somewhere with different feng shui, more suited to the next phase of her life.

Joining the Eight Enrichments to the centre of the Pah Kwa

Mark in the Eight Enrichments and join them to the centre of the Pah Kwa. You should now have a Pah Kwa with eight triangles.

Marking the disturbances

Mark with a cross any disturbance on the outside walls: anywhere that two lines cross over into what should be eight perfect triangles.

Remedies

Use mirrors on any cross on an outside wall that is by a window. On any inside walls you can use plants, water or whatever you intuit to be the necessary remedy.

It is quite interesting to note that both the windows in the study and in the downstairs WC need remedies. You will often find that remedies are needed near windows.

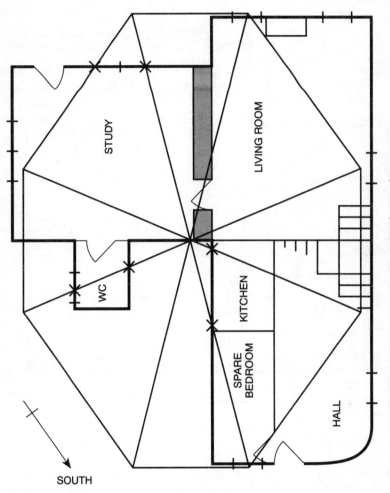

STUDY

LIVING ROOM

WC

KITCHEN

SPARE
BEDROOM

HALL

SOUTH

Fig. 7.3   Ground plan, Pah Kwa, eight triangles and crosses

CASE STUDY 2

Follow exactly the same procedure as for our first case study.

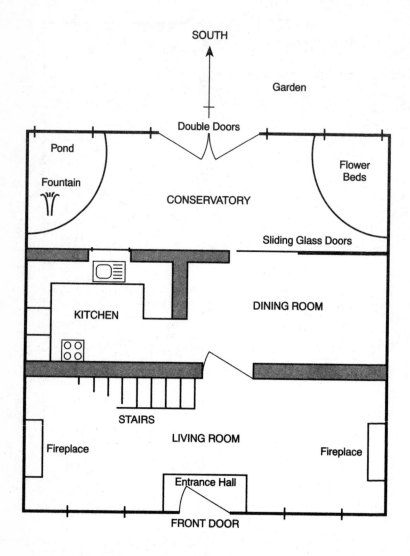

Fig. 7.4   *Ground plan of terraced house*

Ground plan and compass direction

Figure 7.4 shows the ground plan. This house faces due north.

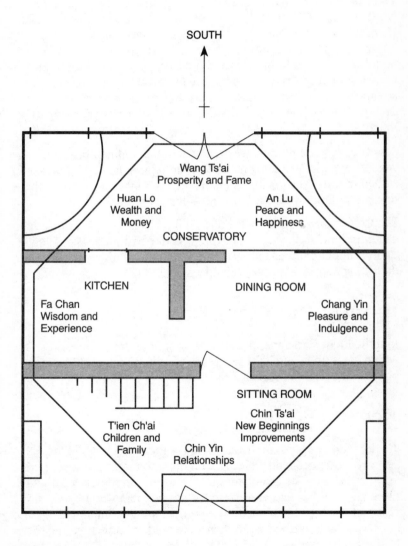

SOUTH

Wang Ts'ai
Prosperity and Fame

Huan Lo
Wealth and
Money

An Lu
Peace and
Happiness

CONSERVATORY

KITCHEN

DINING ROOM

Fa Chan
Wisdom and
Experience

Chang Yin
Pleasure and
Indulgence

SITTING ROOM

Chin Ts'ai
New Beginnings
Improvements

T'ien Ch'ai
Children and
Family

Chin Yin
Relationships

Fig. 7.5 *Terraced house with Pah Kwa*

Overlaying the Pah Kwa shape on the ground plan

You will see from Figure 7.5 that although this house faces north it is still an exceptionally well-balanced house with no missing areas. However, because it faces north we will still have to make some improvements. If you look at where the Enrichments fall you may notice that the wealth/money and prosperity/fame areas both fall in the conservatory – not the best place to encourage worldly advancement. However, the Huan Lo has an extra piece, as does the An Lu – not bad for success despite sitting in the sunshine too much!

Also the pleasure/indulgence area falls in the dining room with the wisdom/experience falling in the kitchen. Do we have the house of someone who likes to eat, entertain friends a lot and generally live a relaxed and indulgent life? You bet – It's my house!

The Chin Ts'ai and the T'ien Ch'ai both have extra bits. Chin Ts'ai is all about new beginnings – new projects like writing books? T'ien Ch'ai is about children. I have three of them, and that's the side of the sitting room where they like to watch TV!

Joining the Eight Enrichments

Join the Eight Enrichments to the centre of the Pah Kwa and mark with a cross anywhere that two lines cross in what should be eight perfect triangles (see Figure 7.6).

Remedies

The kitchen needs four mirrors – I've got them there, while the conservatory needs four remedies on the internal walls – I've gone for plants there. The dining room has a mirror on the back wall and there are a further two mirrors on the sitting room wall by the staircase. The sliding glass door from the dining room to the conservatory presented a problem as I couldn't hang anything there or use a mirror. It was solved by using one of those 3D effect round mirrored designs that stick onto glass.

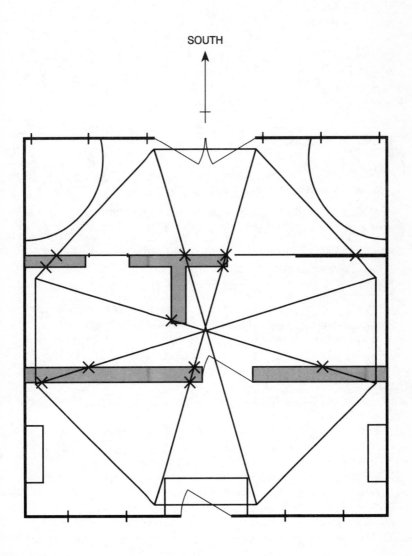

SOUTH

Fig. 7.6 *Terrace with Pah Kwa and triangles and crosses*

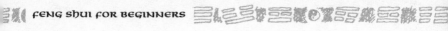

I think the fish pond and fountain in the Huan Lo (wealth and money) area in the conservatory may be starting to work.

We also almost need to turn the house completely around using mirrors on all four outside walls if we want to encourage more worldly advancement. However, it won't be necessary as I am moving to a house that faces south-east, has hills to the north and east, flat ground to the south and west. It has a river that runs down from the north-west and cuts across the bottom of the front garden and disappears off to the south east – complete with waterfalls and bamboo groves. Perfect feng shui!

PRACTICE

- Work out the Inner Good Fortune for your own house and see where you can improve the feng shui.

- Decide on which remedies you need. Implement them and see if you feel any different over a few months.

- Check the furniture placements in your house and adjust as necessary. Monitor the improvements.

- Look at the feng shui of any major government buildings. The White House is a good example: there are three roads forming an arrowed killing ch'i aimed directly at it – interesting!

APPENDIX 1
FENG SHUI AND
THE I CHING

The 64 hexagrams of the I Ching can be used in conjunction with feng shui. Simply look up your compass direction (front door alignment) along the left-hand side of the chart shown on page 100 (Former Heaven Sequence) and the area of Enrichment you want to know about along the top (Later Heaven Sequence). Read off the relevant hexagram. If you want further information you can look up the actual hexagram in a copy of the I Ching.

Later Heaven Sequence - (King Wen)

Former Heaven Sequence - (Fu Hsi)

Enrichment → / Front Door (Compass) ↓	Chin Yin / K'an	T'ien Ch'al / K'en	Fa Chan / Chen	Huan Lo / H'sun	Wang Ts'ai / Li	An Lu / K'un	Chang Yin / Tui	Chin Ts'ai / Ch'ien
Tui SouthEast	Chien Regulations 60	Sun Decrease 41	Kuei Mei Marriage 54	Chung Fu Inmost Sincerity 61	Kuei Disunion 38	Liu Approach 19	Tui Joy 58	Lu Care 10
Ch'ien South	Hsu Waiting 5	Ta Ch'u Tamed 26	Ta Chuang Great 34	Hsiao Ch'u Restraint 9	Ta Yu Abundance 14	Tai Peace 11	Kuai Purifying 43	Ch'en Creative 1
H'sun SouthWest	Ching A Well 48	Ku Arresting Decay 18	Heng Perseverance 32	Sun Gentle Persuasion 57	Ting The Cauldron 50	Sheng Ascending 46	Ta Kuo Excess 28	Kou Encountering 44
K'an West	K'an The Perilous 29	Meng Youthful Inexperience 4	Chieh Freeing 40	Luan Dispersion 59	Wei Chi Ending 64	Shih Force 7	K'un Oppression 47	Sung Conflict 6
K'en NorthWest	Chien Arresting Movement 29	Ken Keeping Still 52	Hsiao Kuo Routine 62	Chien Growth 53	Lu Travel 56	Ch'ion Humility 15	Hsien Influence 31	Tun Retreat 33
K'un North	Pi Union 8	Po Falling Apart 23	Yu Harmony 16	Kuan Contemplation 20	Chin Progress 35	K'un Perceptive 2	Ts'ui Gathering Together 45	Pi Stagnation 12
Chen NorthEast	Chun Initial Difficulty 3	I Nourishment 27	Chen Exciting Power 51	I Increase 42	Shih Ho Biting Through 21	Fu Returning 24	Sui Following 17	Wu Wang Correctness 25
Li East	Chi Chi After Completion 63	Pi Adornment 22	Feng Prosperity 55	Chin Ten The Family 37	Li Clinging 30	Ming I Brightening 36	Ko Revolution 49	Tung Jen Friends 13

Fig. A.1 Feng shui and the I Ching

APPENDIX 2
CHART OF DIRECTIONS
AND FURTHER INFORMATION

			Ken				
Tzu	Promotion	Rat	Water	11 a.m.-1 a.m.	North	January	Aquarius
Ch'ou	Travel	Ox	Metal	1 a.m.-3 a.m.	NNE	February	Pisces
Yin	Energy	Tiger	Fire	3 a.m.-5 a.m.	NE	March	Aries
			H'sun				
Mao	Marriage	Hare	Wood	5 a.m.-7 a.m.	East	April	Taurus
Chen	Sexuality	Dragon	Water	7 a.m.-9 a.m.	SSE	May	Gemini
Ssu	Children	Snake	Metal	9 a.m.-11 a.m.	SE	June	Cancer
			K'un				
Wu	Property	Horse	Fire	11 a.m.-1 p.m.	South	July	Leo
Wei	Family	Sheep	Wood	1 p.m.-3 p.m.	SSW	August	Virgo
Shen	Money	Monkey	Water	3 p.m.-5 p.m.	SW	September	Libra
			Ch'ien				
Yu	Longevity	Cockerel	Metal	5 p.m.-7 p.m.	West	October	Scorpio
Hsu	Friends	Dog	Fire	7 p.m.-9 p.m.	NNW	November	Sagittarius
Hai	Happiness	Pig	Wood	9 p.m.-11 p.m.	NW	December	Capricorn

This chart gives compatibility, times of the day we may feel best at, best house directions, areas of human development that concern us most, comparison of Eastern with Western astrology, etc.

APPENDIX 3
THE FENG SHUI
COMPASS RINGS

The Heaven Plate

1   Trigrams of Former Heaven Sequence
2   Symbols of the nine stars
3   The 24 mountains
4   The eight major planets
5   The 64 hexagrams
6   The 64 hexagrams changing
7   The 24 fortnights of the year
8   The 28 auspicious burial constellations
9   The 360 degrees of the compass
10 The 72 dragon's veins of ch'i
11 Mountains and the dragon's veins

The Human Plate

12 Stems and branches of a person's horoscope
13 The 60 points of good and bad luck
14 The spirit paths of the dead
15 Earth and mountain hexagrams for auspicious sites to live
16 Auspicious sites for burial
17 Division into the five aspects and the horoscope
18 Yin and yang
19 Auspicious river directions
20 Auspicious burial near rivers
21 The dead and ch'i
22 Good and bad positions for burial

The Earth Plate

FURTHER READING

Arcarti, Kristyna, *I Ching for Beginners*, Headway, 1994

Beinfield, Harriet, and Korngold, Efrem, *Between Heaven and Earth*, Ballantine Books, 1991

Bynner, Witter, *The Way of Life*, Perigee Books, 1944

Farrington Hook, Diana, *The I Ching and Mankind*, Routledge & Kegan Paul, 1975

Feuchtwang, Stephen, *An Anthropological Analysis of Chinese Geomancy*, SMC, 1974

Park Boyle, Veolita, *The Fundamental Principles of the Yi-king Tao*, W. & G. Foyle, 1943

Wilhelm, Richard, *The Secret of the Golden Flower*, Routledge & Kegan Paul, 1974

Wing, R. L., *The I Ching Workbook*, Aquarian, 1983

GLOSSARY

An Lu South-west direction, peace and happiness
Arrowed killing ch'i three straight lines of ch'i converging to a point

Chai dwelling, houses
Chang Yin west, pleasure and indulgence, dangerous
Chen The Arousing
Ch'i energy
Ch'ien The Creative
Chin metal
Chin Ts'ai north-west, new beginnings
Chin Yin north, relationships

Enrichments the Eight areas of life situations

Fa Chan east, wisdom and experience
Fan ch'i offensive ch'i, residual emotions
Fang inner
Feng wind
Feng Huang the Red Phoenix of the south
Feng shui wind/water, Chinese geomancy
Feng shui hsien-sheng a feng shui consultant or practitioner

Hsin heart, ourselves
Hsueh surroundings
H'sun the wind
Huan Lo south east, wealth
Huo fire

I Ching the Book of Changes

K'an The Dangerous
Ken The Stillness
Killing ch'i ch'i flowing too fast in a straight line
K'un The Receptive

Li The Clinging
Liu trees, gardens, willows
Lo-p'an the feng shui compass
Lo Shu the magic square
Lung mei the dragon's veins, paths of ch'i

Mu wood

Pah Kwa the great symbol (yin/yang symbol with the Eight trigrams)

Sha unhealthy ch'i
Sha ch'i disruptive ch'i from the west
Shan mountains
Shan shui mountains and water, style of Chinese landscape painting
Sheng ch'i growing ch'i from the east
Shui water

T'ai Ch'i the Supreme Ultimate
T'ai chi chu'an Chinese martial art
Tao the Way, a religion, philosophy, way of life, the Universal
    Principle
T'ien ch'ai north-east, children and family
T'sang ch'i hidden ch'i from the north
Ts'ang feng cold hidden wind that blows from hollows and can
    cause ill health
T'u earth
Tui The Lake

Wang Ts'ai south, prosperity and fame
Wen the Green Dragon of the East
Wu the White Tiger of the West
Wu Hsing the five aspects or elements

Yang creative energy
Yang ch'i nourishing ch'i from the south
Yin receptive energy
Yuan Wu the Black Tortoise of the North

Titles in this series

Angels
Astral Projection
Astrology
Astrology and Health
Becoming Prosperous
Body and Mind Reading
Chakras
Channelling
Chinese Horoscopes
Crystal Healing
Dowsing
Dream Interpretation
Earth Mysteries
Enlightenment
Feng Shui
Freeing Your Intuition
Gems and Crystals
Ghosts
The Goddess
Graphology
The Healing Powers of Plants
Herbs for Magic and Ritual
I Ching
Interpreting Signs and Symbols
The Language of Flowers
Love Signs
The Magic and Mystery of Trees
Meditation
Mediumship
Money Signs
The Moon and You
Norse Tradition
Numerology
Numerology and Relationships
Pagan Gods for Today's Man
Paganism

Palmistry
Qabalah
Reiki
Reincarnation and You
Runes
Seeing the Future
Sex Signs
Shamanism
Some Traditional African Beliefs
Spells and Rituals
Spiritual Healing
Star Signs
Tantric Sexuality
Tarot
Visualisation
Witchcraft
Working With Colour
Your Psychic Powers